stop
check
go.

About the Author

'Ditch' Townsend was born to missionary doctors in Thailand in 1966, going to boarding school in Malaysia and Surrey, then day school after his parents returned to the UK in 1980. He married Christine in 1990 and they have three children—Asher (b.1991), Esther (b.1993) and Joel (b.1995). He qualified in Medicine in 1991 and thankfully gave this up after becoming fully registered in 1992.

Since then, he has enjoyed managing the setting up and operations of the Tear Fund (UK) Short Term Overseas Programmes (STOP) Unit. He resigned from this at the end of 1994, to prepare for a three year training management job back 'home' in Malaysia, in the sphere of AIDS counselling, seconded by Tear Fund (UK). He has travelled in Europe, Central America, sub-Saharan Africa, the Middle East and Southeast Asia. He has been involved in providing Critical Incident Debriefings to over 30 emergency relief staff, including a visit to provide psychological support to missionaries and staff from a number of organisations, following massacres in Burundi in 1993.

His growing interest is in support structures for Christians involved in 'a-typical' cross-cultural ministries: tentmakers, missionaries with inadequate organisational support, those sent to work overseas by their employers, relief and development workers, etc.

stop check go.

A Short-Term Overseas Projects Checklist
A practical guide for cross-cultural teamwork

'DITCH' TOWNSEND

OM
publishing

OM Publishing is an imprint of Paternoster Publishing,
P.O. Box 300, Carlisle, Cumbria CA3 0QS, U.K.

The Author and The Publisher disclaim any liability for any situation
arising from taking any explicit or implicit advice in the text: through
inadequacies in the Author's knowledge and judgement, or due to
changes since its writing, or any other errors. This book was written to
highlight important areas for further investigation and preparation by its
Readers: hence its extensive note pages. Each Reader should take the
trouble to follow up each category as it applies to him/herself, relying on
their own responses to the book's challenges (written in the notes
perhaps). The book was partly written precisely because so many
programme Organisers and Participants appear to be insufficiently
prepared; it was not designed to remove the responsibility of preparation.
In particular, the Medical section and Emergency sections all strongly
advise more adequate, in-depth preparation in advance, than is offered
here.

British Library Cataloguing in Publication Data

A catalogue record for this book is available from the British Library

ISBN 1–85078–240–7

Typeset by Photoprint, Torquay, Devon
and Printed in the U.K. by Guernsey Press Ltd.

Dedicated

To all those who, like me, were damaged by a Short Term experience overseas.

Also to the future of the fledgling Short Term Functional Group of the Evangelical Missionary Alliance in the hope this will provide training, support, research, updates and leadership in the field of Short Term Mission. And that accredited membership by churches, missions and new organisers, will offer participants safety of mind, knowing that adequate preparations have been made and procedures put in place, to ensure their trip is the best it could be.

Acknowledgements

Overwhelmingly, to Christine, who encouraged me in writing this in the run up to a three year overseas job; including two moves, a house redecoration, two months without income, four weeks when I was away training, several months with her parents, a sold car, her own correspondence course, a three year old, a one year old and a baby half way through this! Thanks also for her input on the section relating to **Personal Spiritual Issues** and **Language**.

Also, to Jennifer Loughlin, former Personnel Director at Tear Fund, who put up with my untimely resignation from one job to allow a break before the next.

Next, to Stanley Davies, Executive Director of the Evangelical Missionary Alliance; Paul Lindsay, Director of the Christian Service Centre; Dave Pope, Director of Saltmine Trust—and others who offered their encouragement and support in this initiative.

Lastly, without whom this book would have no practical basis: to all who have come through their experience under the guidance of Tear Fund's Short Term Overseas Programmes Unit and its varying staff whilst I've been there: Jane Eldridge, Jill Hanton, Julia Latter, Ruth Devane, and Naomi Vinen.

Contents

Yes, if you have *any* association with Short Term overseas opportunities.

WHAT SORT OF TRIPS?

Specifically:

- It is about *Team trips*.
- It is about very short trips, several *weeks* or *months long*.
- It is for *Christians*.

More generally:

- The mine of information may also help people involved with longer projects of *six months or more*.
- Whilst it does not specifically cover *Teams involving parental consent*, there are many practical topics which could be of benefit.
- Much of the guide could be useful for *educational* and *non-religious* projects.
- *Lone travellers* are partly catered for, some sections will interest them.

WHAT KIND OF READERS?

Participants – The first section has you in mind. It helps you think through why you might want to go. It tells you how to find the right programme and apply. It goes on to practical issues in preparing. What should you expect and how will you cope? It provides useful tips for making the most of your time whilst overseas. Finally, it prepares you for your return and helps you think about your future. (NB By reading later sections, you can also see many of the questions the Organisers and Leaders should be addressing).

Leaders – The second section is to help prepare for some of the special concerns you face, including styles of leadership, group dynamics, discipline and managing crises.

Organisers – The third section is for you, whether representing an Organisation, church, college group, etc. How do you go about running one of these trips? Who's responsible? Should you work in partnership with anyone? How do you plan the programme? Are legal issues understood? How can you select the right Participants and Leaders? How will you prepare them or follow them up? Could you handle an emergency? Is this the best time or place to be operating?

Overseas Hosts – There is a final section for you. If you have no experience of this sort of thing then this will orientate you to some of the issues which are often taken for granted, but frequently misunderstood on both sides!

MEMOS

What sort of trip are you interested in?

What is your potential involvement with it?

There are already many publications which are very helpful when planning trips overseas. Some are mentioned in the text in the relevant sections. A guide to some useful resources is given at the end of this book, though none of them aims to do what this book does.

FORMAT

This book is designed:

– With blank pages for you to record planning notes.
– To cover most core areas of preparation. You can centre your plans on the 200+ topics (not comprehensively though, because of the special nature of your plans).
– To help practical planning by compressing text, so you can scan issues rapidly. I have limited all relevant discussion to one spread per topic.
– To take a workbook approach. Since it does not answer every question raised, you can tailor your plans to meet your own objectives. Also I can paint a broad picture of Short Term Programmes, without writing an encyclopaedia!
– To identify key resources for answering questions which are too specific for this guide, e.g. the local climate and culture.
– With extensive section checklists to help you prepare.

READERSHIP

Participants
Read the section written for you to aid your preparation. Make notes to help you when you are overseas. Read the section for Hosts to see how your arrival might be being viewed. On return, Review your experience using the last few pages of your section. **If you are unsure about how much thought the Organisers have put into the trip, review their section and ask them appropriate questions!**

Leaders
Read everything. It's a privilege to be asked to lead, but don't allow that to cloud sound judgement. Has preparation been adequate in the light of what you've read? Can you fulfill what's being asked of you?

Organisers
Read everything, prepare thoroughly, postpone if necessary, be responsible.

Overseas Hosts
Read the section written for you. If you need more time to think or seek advice before receiving people, say so well in advance. It

usually takes a long time to plan a trip and delays near the time can actually mean cancellation. It may help you to understand what those coming or organising the trip might think and feel, if you read the sections written for them.

MEMOS

What might you use the book for?

Which parts will be most useful?

MISGUIDANCE

'**No preparation needed: we're Christians.**' This seems to me, to reflect the attitude of some Christians who get involved in Short Term overseas work. This is a twisted paraphrase of Romans 8:28. I wonder how many are so misguided?

Perhaps they translate the saying, 'Don't just sit there: do something,' as, '**There's no time to think: just act.**' This may seem excusable in the light of the crises we hear about, not least when they are within driving distance e.g. Eastern Europe.

MOTIVATION

My intention is not to accuse readers of deliberate mismanagement, nor even of avoidable negligence (a close relation). I understand the pressures many of us face to act now. Perhaps you struggle with guilt as I did. Allied to this is patronising pity. But the purest motivation is love.

FAITH VERSUS PREPARATION

Whatever the motivation, it should not push us to operate on faith alone, but to include an adequate measure of thought. There are countless examples through history of Christians who went forward in what they considered 'faith' and got it wrong, as there are of Christians who excluded faith and messed up. The balance will vary and with it, the definition of 'an adequate measure'. But I would argue that 'faith' is most likely a gift from God when it is most necessary! The converse is: if you know it would be simple to obtain appropriate advice, why expect God to plant instant knowledge and understanding in your head, or to guide you 'one step at a time', blindfold on a well-marked path through a minefield?

I believe we can no longer excuse ourselves on the grounds of ignorance and throw ourselves on God's grace, when it comes to Short Term overseas work. We can expect tragedies and near-misses whenever we step into the unknown. It is for this reason that I draw strength from Romans 8:28. But there is now enough in the store of common experience and resources, for us all to anticipate many of the problems well in advance.

However we need faith—and not only as the spur to action! I might criticise procedures, but I would be more hesitant about criticising programme types and venues. There are important lessons to learn about such issues as sustainability, partnership and personal safety, which are examined in this book. But having thought them through adequately and sought wise advice, you must hold firm in your faith, if you truly feel God's call to something which is not currently 'flavour of the month' amongst academics, peers or opinion leaders.

MEMOS

What do you expect to learn from this book?

CURRENT MEMBERS

Short Term overseas Mission is not new, but recently the UK has seen a phenomenal increase in the numbers on such programmes. Data from various Organisations in 1992 suggested that since 1985, the numbers of participants had increased sevenfold, almost doubling every two years.[1] I estimate that 1994 saw 1,500 people from the UK on programmes with established Missions and 500 to 1,000 on trips organised by churches or newer para-church groups.

VERY SHORT TERMERS

The predominant group, with most of the following features. Up to 3 months abroad; no career break. Team-based, no language study, participants pay, minimal skills, no Bible training, single participants. Our research[2] implies that:

- Half the Returners go overseas again, Short or Long Term.
- Of this half, nine tenths go overseas into Christian work and nine tenths to the 'Third World'.
- A quarter go to work for a while in Not-For-Profit Organisations (NFPOs); three quarters of these for Christian ones.
- Two fifths of Returners become NFPO representatives; over four fifths of these for Christian ones.

'GAPPERS'

Typically – Over 6 months abroad; career break; individuals; limited language study; variable financing; work matches experience; Bible training optional; no children. Research[3] suggests:

- Two thirds feel dependent on their previous experience.
- Half feel they have a reasonable amount of responsibility (one quarter have too much, one fifth too little).
- Relationships with nationals and UK staff are positive, but up to a fifth find relationships with Missionaries and work supervisors are negative.
- One third feel work supervision is poor.
- Three quarters expect to work overseas subsequently.
- Key needs highlighted: accurate preparatory information, adequate project arrangements, avoiding departure delays, basic language study, more support from home whilst overseas, opportunity to extend placements and adequate support on return.

LONG TERMERS

Frequently: 3–4 year 'terms'; estranged from career path; job hierarchy; longer language study; long-term funding; job description; Bible training; mature singles or families. Research[4] indicates:

- Of those aged 20–30, 31–50 and 51+: three fifths, two fifths and one fifth respectively worked Short Term first.
- Two fifths who went Short Term were there less than 3 months.

MIXED GROUP

A fourth group shows a range of all the features above.

MEMOS

List the key traits of your trip:

1 *'Ditch' Townsend*, 'Overview of Short Term Programmes up to 1992' in: Proceedings of a Meeting of Christian Short Term Overseas Programme Organisers, 1992, Tear Fund, p.8–12. [OVERVIEW]
2 *'Ditch' Townsend, Jane Eldridge, Julia Latter*, Short Termers—Survey of Tear Fund (UK) Short Term Overseas Volunteers Between 1972 and 1990. Tear Fund, 1994. [SHORT TERMERS]
3 *Jill Hanton*, Internal (Tear Fund 1994).
4 *Sandra Kimber*, SHORT TERMERS pp. 20–23.

FUTURE NUMBERS

Without changes, Applicant numbers can't continue to rise much more. To continue filling places with mostly 'first-timers' will be a challenge, given the big increase in programmes on offer. Four pieces of anecdotal evidence suggest that Applicants and not Organisers are becoming the main ones picking and choosing:

1. Virtually every University Christian student who could go, is being reached by someone each year.
2. Tear Fund found that Spanish-speaking Applicants were saturated with opportunities and fewer applied or accepted places on Latin America projects.
3. We were increasingly being approached by Missions wanting our rejected Applicants to fill their programmes.
4. Our research[1] suggests that Participants are increasingly seeing Short Term Mission as an end in itself, not just a preparation for Long Term work. Organisations resisting this will be passed over by some Applicants.

FUTURE OPPORTUNITIES

Established Missions. Some are trimming their programmes. Specialisation is an option. Another is to market programmes aggressively with 'price wars', targeted promotion, etc. Others are reversing years of ambivalence to Short Term work, now offering these potential supporters a programme.

Church and para-church groups. A threshold seems to have been reached. Eastern Europe's proximity isn't the only factor reducing the threshold for action. Increasingly, groups sense that 'Third World' programmes are possible on an amateur basis, partly due to increasing international mobility and communications. The fact that few Missions have been willing to help them may fuel this. Some returning Short-Termers encourage a belief in amateur abilities.

Marketing. If Organisations don't wish to compete, various attitudes and possibilities will need modifying and exploring. Some may need to recognise redundancies in their approach; places could be reduced and specialised programmes handled. Others may choose to 'market' programmes at the expense of other Organisers. Collaboration is an option too.

Diversification. Furthermore, thought could be given to bringing new non-student groups into the Short Term scene: around a quarter of Tear Fund's Applicants are now over 25. Workers need shorter projects; teachers can often only go in August; retired people can be invaluable. A few Organisations make opportunities for under-18s, though legal issues can be considerable. Lastly, some groups are placing people from overseas in the UK.

MEMOS

What are your attitudes to Short Term Mission?

1 SHORT TERMERS.

ATTITUDES

Colonialism. At first, Mission was as much associated with Western civilisation as with Christian religion. 'Alexander Duff ... the founding father of educational Mission in India, believed that Western science and English literature would undermine the cultural confidence of Hindus in such a way that the whole edifice of Hinduism would crumble and the nation would turn to Christ'.[1] The dedication needed to pass on a whole new way of life, meant that 'Short Termism' received short shrift from the Mission establishment. This period saw the rise of evangelical champions of the poor and the oppressed.[2]

Anti-Colonialism. The shift to anti-colonialism and pluralism brought a confusion of Mission approaches. Some made guilty attempts to atone for their forebears: 'Partnerships' became idealised and every request for resources went unquestioned.[3] Still others ignored requests from developing world churches in the sixties, for a brief moratorium on Mission to enable them to build independent, non-Western foundations. This phase also saw the separation (still present in many Christians' minds) of evangelism from social action, the latter tending to become a dirty word.

Though many Missions persist with older patterns (and some newer Missions even have a colonial mentality).[3] the reflections of pluralism in much of Mission today are striking. 'We do not seem to want to impose on others some coercive ideology, but instead are prepared to listen more, appreciate more, participate more, dialogue more'.[1]

Post Anti-Colonialism. The above agenda is now appreciated by many 'Developing World' churches, whose younger adults remember little of colonialism and don't foster anti-colonialist feelings. These so called 'post anti-colonialists' have no need of Western guilt and seek partners to help share the Gospel, rather than to be manipulated into believing Western resources will always be a prerequisite.[3]

THEOLOGY

This last and current phase has seen many Christians reexamining their understanding of the Gospel. Rejoining the split between evangelism and social action, they aim for the whole Gospel which Jesus came to proclaim to the poor, captives, blind and oppressed (Luke 4:18).[2]

Short Term work fits with several biblical insights on Mission:[1]
- **Urgency** (Luke 10)
- **Involvement in a** process **of salvation** (John 4:31–38)
- **The value of 'outsiders'**—e.g. Moses, Amos and Jonah
- **Apprenticeship** (Luke 10; Mark 6:37–44)

MEMOS

Write down what you would change, add or emphasise regarding Attitudes and Theology:

1 *Jonathan Ingleby*, 'Theological Reflections on Short Term Mission' in: Proceedings of a Meeting of Christian Short Term Overseas Programme Organisers, Tear Fund, 1992, p.3–7.
2 *Tim Chester*, Awakening To A World Of Need, 1993, Inter Varsity Press, Leicester.
3 *Vinay Samuel*, Presentation at a conference on Personnel For Partnership In Post Anti-Colonial Mission, 1993, Oxford Centre For Mission Studies.

If given a 'correct' answer to this question, when interviewing, I don't take it at face value. There are typically two or more sides to each response, which I have tried to illustrate below.

GIVING

- *I want to help poor people.* Unskilled with no idea of the local environment, culture, and language? The trip's cost can often support several labourers' families for months.
- *I want to be a witness of Jesus to locals.* Most Christians are not Westerners and know their own cultures better than you. Their zeal often shames us. Can you do better?

RECEIVING

- *I want to grow as a Christian.* Are you prepared for the pain of shattered illusions? These trips can be very challenging.
- *I want to see life in the 'Third World'; I want to learn.* Without involvement, will you gain? Is it Poverty Tourism?
- *I want to get away from the badness of my own culture, to a better one.* Everywhere, some cultural things are bad. Rosy spectacles will eventually disillusion you.
- *I'm taking some time out to travel.* How might locals overseas feel, knowing you have more to spend on a holiday than a whole family's yearly income?
- *It's for training or work experience.* You'll find things tough enough, without also feeling obliged to go. Also, are you prepared to compromise a lot to fit into local practices, if necessary?
- *To meet Mr/Miss 'Right'!* Any intense relationship can seriously disrupt Team dynamics and culturally appropriate witness. Are you prepared to wait till you get home?

CALLING

- *I believe God has called me to go Short Term.* Selectors may disagree. They can get it wrong, but maybe you can.
- *I want to test the possibility that God may be calling me overseas longer term.* Why not apply longer term then? Are you afraid, or looking for grounds to disagree?

EXTERNAL PRESSURES

- *Everyone else does it; I don't want to be left out.* It may be 'flavour of the month', but is that a reason?
- *I'm feeling pressured into going.* Then don't go. Or maybe your eyes do need opening or your complacency shattering.

MISCELLANEOUS

– *I want to visit a situation I already have links with.* This implies power. Could someone there visit you? If not, are there adequate balances or is there dominance and patronage?
– *I'm not sure, I just want to.* How can you measure success without a goal? Or would anything be an improvement for you?

MEMOS

Note your reasons for wanting to go, including positive arguments and drawbacks to each one.

AIMS AND OBJECTIVES

Some people jump straight in at the deep end, picking without thinking. Maybe a friend persuaded you to apply. You will get most from a trip, knowing your Aims and setting out towards them. Work through the following process first. (Even if already committed, don't pre-judge its conclusion.)

1. *Establish appropriate Aims*
   See the preceding page for guidance. There could be all sorts of possibilities. Objectives are usually more fully achievable and measurable. Keep Aims much more open, e.g. I want wider gastronomic experience.
2. *Set some Objectives*
   These should be Specific, Measurable, Achievable, Realistic and Timed (SMART, a widely known strategic planning acronym). e.g. I want to experience authentic Mongolian cuisine within two years.
3. *Set some Targets*
   These should arise directly out of the Objectives and not introduce new ones. An early Target should be adequate research. e.g. Within two weeks, I will have telephoned two travel agents for quotes on flights to Mongolia.
4. *Review progress regularly.*
   You will need to redefine Targets and maybe Objectives or even Aims, in the light of developments. e.g. I have discovered there is a Mongolian Barbecue restaurant in Twickenham. My new target is to make a booking there and obtain a refund on my return ticket to Ulan Bator.

Few are as pedantic as all this implies. But to follow it through initially, will help you tune your thinking. It will also guide you at interview, with searching questions.

Everyone offering programmes should have their own Aims and Objectives, one being the programme itself. It would be wise to ensure that you understand why they are running it. Then you can measure the degree of match between it and you. NB This will arm you with a quiver of questions, when at the interview you are asked, 'Do you want to ask us anything?'

FINDING PROGRAMMES

In the Short Term Service Directory, published by the Christian Service Centre, there are 35 kinds of programme mentioned, in every region of the world.[1]

Broadly speaking, there are Specialist volunteer programmes and three kinds of Unskilled volunteer programme: Spiritual, Practical and Mixed. There is sometimes a tension here.

Another general division is between External/Western managed (Implementing) and Local/Indigenous managed (Secondment) programmes.

Organisers can also be split between those with only Short-Termers (mostly newer set ups) and those with wider remits.

MEMOS

Outline your Aims:

Outline your Objectives:

Outline and review successive Targets:

1.

2.

3.

What are the most appropriate Programme types?

1 Their address is: Holloway Street West, Lower Gormal, Dudley, W. Midlands, DY3 2DZ (01902 882836).

Selection is usually less than ideal. Its apparent success often depends on there being lots of 'good' Applicants. If going isn't the best thing for you yet, it may not come out at selection. Applicants sometimes tell me that if they are selected by me, then it must be God's will. I agree that God will ultimately work all things together for good. I do not agree that I act always under God's inspiration. *I can make mistakes about people's lives.*

SELF-SELECTION CRITERIA

Rather than simply 'pushing doors' to see if any open, examine yourself using some of the criteria selectors may try to use. This could also ease their job; you will answer better or not apply at all.

– Evangelical Christian Organisations usually require like-minded Participants, regularly attending a like-minded church. Do they? Are you? Find out.
– There may be other excluding criteria, such as age etc. Read promotional literature carefully.
– Many non-Western cultures, not least their churches, are less tolerant than the pluralist West. There may be issues for unmarried people living together, practising homosexuals, divorcees, separated couples, those admitting to a history of unmarried sexual experience and those with a criminal record. If in doubt, seek advice from an appropriate source, such as the Christian Service Centre, or from Organisations you may wish to apply to.
– Sometimes, non-Western cultures are intolerant of any physical expression of male/female relationships. Seek advice from the Organisers, before applying with your fiancée or girl/boyfriend.
– Would you be unable to fit with the published dates for selection, flights, reunion etc? Do you expect to be able to travel independently at the end? If so, contact the Organiser before applying. They may say no immediately.
– 'Third World' environments, communications and facilities can be less than rudimentary. If you have a disability, can you travel and care for yourself independently? If not, contact the Organiser before applying. Some project venues may be better able to cope than others.
– If you have a medical problem which could be triggered, made worse or could need unavailable treatment, you should seek appropriate medical advice before applying. Diarrhoea alone is very common and can lead to dehydration, over-complicating a number of conditions.

- Do you know why you're applying (see previous sections) and do you have a reasonable idea of what to expect overseas? If not, find out first. (Read this book?)
- These overseas trips can be very stressful. It is wise not to add to this. Are you already stressed? Have you experienced a major loss in the last six months? Do you have a history of treated depression or mental illness? If so, you would do well to seek advice from a qualified counsellor, mental health professional or general practitioner before applying.

MEMOS

Note any relevant positive and negative criteria. (On balance, should you apply?)

FORMAL SYSTEMS

Research demonstrates the inadequacy of interviews alone, not least unstructured ones. Most selectors have application forms and references; some more diverse systems. Specific, relevant application forms and references are better than interview alone. Some selectors underestimate the value of prior self–selection, given positive programme outcomes.

INFORMAL SYSTEMS

For some, particularly in churches etc, selection is less formal. *Advantages*: You may be known to fit the Aims of the trip. Planning, raising support, training, overseas support and personal follow up are also easier. *Disadvantages*: You might be included (or not) due to personalities, not ability. Also, the trip may be affected by availability of skills.

TIMING

Closing dates can be six months or more in advance. (Enquire about July trips before Christmas if possible.) If rejected early, you'll have more time to hunt down other options.

CORRESPONDENCE

Make your own enquiries and handle your own letters. It demonstrates initiative, personal interest and commitment.

APPLICATION FORMS

These should be legible. Highlight skills and experience; don't keep information till a hoped-for interview. Forms, which are reviewed systematically in large numbers, should not be replaced by, or cross-refer to a cv.

DEPOSITS

A deposit (non-returnable deposits unless you are rejected) may be requested. It complicates your attempts at multiple applications but is easier for Organisers, who know that fewer offers will be turned down. Also, it can reduce applications to oversubscribed programmes.

REFERENCES

References should be handled as soon as feasible (faster if possible!) Some are needed before the application is considered, others before confirming a place.

INTERVIEWS

Interviews take many forms. Dress conservatively unless told otherwise; would you easily offend sensitivities overseas? Know why you want to go and why you suit this programme. Understand what you're letting yourrself in for. What are your skills and weaknesses (practical and personal)? Be confident and think out some searching questions.

SELECTION COURSES

These are rare, modelling more complex, accurate systems. They rely on observing behaviour during team games, conflict resolution etc. A tiny number add leadership exercises, individual initiative and sleep deprivation!

MEMOS

Draw and keep updating a timetable for each Organisation you are applying to. (Underline deadlines):

FAMILY

Your desire to go overseas can induce a whole range of reactions from your extended family. Think about this early on. At its best, they will offer you tremendous support, encouragement, finance and prayer. At its worst, they may feel abandoned, rejected, angry, depressed, afraid, used, cynical, embittered. You may be surprised at the strength of feeling which emerges if you just raise the possibility, let alone announce your imminent departure as their first inkling of it. Try to anticipate and plan the process. If appropriate, involve them from the 'possible idea' stage, through choosing where to go, to final preparations. If you are leaving a spouse or a dependant, then consider your responsibilities: should you be leaving?

FRIENDS

Friendships depend on respect and honesty. Involvement in your decision making can be very positive. A friend's advice may be right on the nail. Who knows you better? If you are 'going steady' or engaged, remember that a separation may be a very trying time. Can the relationship stand it? Do you have a hidden agenda? Say what needs to be said before going. (I don't know how my girlfriend forgave me for writing to her from Uganda to break it off. A friend used his fiancée's visit to him in Africa, as an opportunity to do the same.)

CHRISTIAN FELLOWSHIP

For most this means a church, though for some more itinerant students, it might be their Christian Union. A corporate body of Christians, willing to pray and stay with you, is invaluable (and essential for selection for many Programmes). They should be a source of formal advice, guidance and reference, from the leadership. They can benefit as a body, from the education inherent in what you learn and share. They ought also to benefit from your involvement on return, with motivation, experience and ideas about mission. They can sometimes provide a willing source of finance.

ORGANISERS

You and they will benefit immeasurably, from your knowing their Aims, Objectives and wider range of activities. You may well be asked about these overseas. Know also, their organisational set up and relevant policies and procedures. Sometimes Organisers help with various practical issues such as visas, work permits, plane tickets. Most importantly, I contend that they should provide you with a basic range of facilities, without which you should be wary. These include reasonable: legal and insurance anticipation; programme design and execution; planning and back-up for emergencies; selection procedures; Participant preparation; leadership; supportive follow up. There could also be a regional support group for the Organisation, who may 'adopt' you.

MEMOS

What reactions do you expect from people?

Do the Organisers come up to standard?

EXPENDITURE

Most programmes require you to raise your costs. Organisers include various items in the cover price (e.g. £1,300 might cover a Londoner on an 8-week trip to Africa, with a £1,000 brochure price including the Direct Costs *starred below, plus a proportion of Indirect Costs, but excluding voluntary funds needed for Overseas Direct Costs):

Personal Direct Costs

UK Travel	Preparatory Materials*
Personal Clothing	Personal Insurance*
Orientation Course*	Vaccinations/Antimalarials/
Air Tickets*	Medicals
Airport Taxes*	Visas/Work Permits*
Local Overseas Travel*	Language Courses
Overseas Accommodation*	Overseas Food/Cooking*
Personal Spending Money	Outings/Safaris
	Reunion Costs

Indirect Costs

Home Administration	Leader's Costs
Overseas Administration	Organiser's Insurance/Legal Advice

Overseas Direct Costs

Tools	Work Materials
Transport/Logistics	Additional Labour/Supervision

INCOME SOURCES

Personal Savings, Overtime, Additional Income.
Overdrafts and Official Loans. Is this really worth it?
Family and Friendly Loans. Consider potential damage to important relationships if you're unable to pay these off.
Trusts and Grant-making bodies. Ask at your library. Apply well in advance and personalise applications (20–100?!)
Previous Educational Establishments. These may be happy to make a small gift or grant to ex-students.
Church. Besides prayer and guidance, your church may be willing to offer you some financial support. Talk to your church Leader or someone involved in its Finance or Mission committee.
Workplace. It is astonishing, the support employers often give, if asked. This can extend to long periods of unpaid leave. Approach your Personnel head.
Fund raising events. These may include sponsored events, jumble sales etc. Check out by-laws restricting street and door to door collecting with your local council.

Local Newspapers. Though not a direct source of funds, most local papers will include a pre-departure story on you, with a request to send donations via them. Write a press release. It should be on one side of A4, double spaced, with **'Press Release'** at the top and your name and address. Keep it brief, active, positive, factually correct and personalised. Avoid confidential information or critical statements about your destination. A black and white photo is an invaluable addition, perhaps of you in a preparatory pose, with a caption on the back.

MEMOS

What will you pay and what will it cover?

How much more might you spend?

What is the total you must raise?

Note fund raising methods, including useful contacts and addresses:

PASSPORT

You require one to re-enter the UK. Application forms from a Post Office, should go in at least one month before visa applications. Phone a Passport Office for urgent ones. Carry ten identical spare passport photos overseas and a photocopy of the 'Particulars' page separately. Make sure your passport is valid for six months beyond your return date.

VISA AND WORK PERMIT

Most countries require you to have a visa before arriving. The process may take up to a month. If your Organisation isn't handling it, talk to a visa handling service, travel agent or the relevant embassy. Be wary of mentioning the word 'work' or 'Christian', on forms. Check on receipt, that the visa will not run out before you return. If going for more than a few weeks, find out from overseas if a work permit will be needed and where it should be applied for.

INSURANCE

Your Organisation may have already sorted this out. If so, don't get your own, as dual cover of a claim is complex. If not, travel agents, insurance brokers or banks can help. Make sure the fine print will not exclude your intentions. A 'round the world' type may suit. For reciprocal healthcare in the EC: apply for an E111 from Post Offices, but also get insured.

MEDICAL CERTIFICATES

For many countries, you are advised to have certain immunisations and antimalarials. Some insist that you show a current certificate for immunisations such as Yellow Fever, Typhoid and even Cholera (despite its ineffectiveness). Keep them with you on arrival. It saves being delayed or immunised on entry and who knows whether the syringe and needle are sterilised (see the section on AIDS)? Few countries require proof of a negative HIV test. You can get advice on vaccines and antimalarials from some GPs, Interhealth, Thomas Cook or British Airways travel centres.

DUTY FREE

UK—Declare and show receipts for most things you've bought outside the EC, especially electrical goods (use the Red channel for advice). Duty free allowances are listed at airports. Also declare any local fruit, vegetables, seeds or meat products. (Full details come with your new Passport.)

Overseas—You might occasionally have to pay a hefty, refundable deposit to bring in expensive electrical equipment. Filming equipment, beyond a camcorder, sometimes needs a special permit. Ask at the embassy.

ILLICIT GOODS

These include controlled drugs and endangered animals, including insects (dead or alive) and their products, for which a permit would be required. Virtually any ivory, turtle, snakeskin or fur fits this category. The DoE suggest that you avoid buying *any* animal product overseas. Beware of being asked to carry goods through customs on behalf of a friendly fellow passenger (smuggler?).

MEMOS

Note personal updates below:

PASSPORT

VISA

WORK PERMIT

INSURANCE

MEDICAL CERTIFICATES

DUTIABLE ITEMS

NATIONAL INSURANCE

If abroad for more than a few months as a volunteer, or paid to go, read the leaflet, Social Security Abroad, NI38, from the DSS. There may be benefits as a Volunteer Development Worker.

TAX

If paid and overseas for at least a year, you might not need to pay tax. Your Organisation may be aware of this. If not, talk to a tax adviser. Obtain form P85 from your tax office.

POWER OF ATTORNEY

If you are working overseas for several months and if you couldn't be contacted easily, it would be wise to sign a Power of Attorney authorising someone to act on your behalf for taxes, banks and other legal issues.

WILL

You might find yourself exposed to additional personal risk. Consider this seriously, not least if you have dependants or assets. Seek legal advice. Remember the value of legacies to charities. The Evangelical Alliance has a useful 'Will Pack'.

VOTING

Even if overseas, you can vote in UK elections for 12 months from 16th February, provided you registered to vote before the previous 10th October (15th September in Northern Ireland). See the leaflet, 'Keeping your vote when living abroad' and form RPF37, from Electoral Registration offices.

CHILD BENEFIT

This can usually be maintained for up to seven weeks after the child leaves the country. Check with the Child Benefit Office.

OTHER BENEFITS

You are liable to lose entitlements if overseas more than a short period of time. Check with the authorities before making plans.

DOMESTIC SERVICES AND CREDIT CARD BILLS

Arrange for payment while absent. Use standing orders, or a friend to pay bills via Power of Attorney or arrangement with your bank, providing direct access to your account.

RENTING AND MORTGAGES

If you will rely on rental income, plan for unrented periods. You will need an agent. A letting agency may be useful, though they will cost around 10% of the rent. Remember to have someone trusted with access to extra funds on your behalf, in case repairs are urgently needed. Talk to your mortgage company and insurers about the best way to arrange payments, to take into account any increases.

COURTS, PROBATION, BAIL, FINES

Don't appear to be escaping legal problems.

MEMOS

Note personal updates for each section, below:

ONE-WAY

Letters and Parcels may or may not arrive, after six months, particularly surface mail. Aerogrammes and postcards do best. Registered services may be unreliable or not exist.

By hand is much depended on by Missionaries. Items should not be sealed, or dutiable. Don't carry items for strangers.

Courier services are the fastest, reliable public service between major cities, but may not have reliable 'up country' deliveries. Items usually should not be dutiable.

Shipping agents can provide advice and service. Air freight is much cheaper than excess baggage, but it may take two weeks (sea will take up to ten weeks). Items need collecting on arrival and should be clearly marked. A knowledgeable local can sometimes help negotiate round delays.

Telegrams/Telemessages – enquire at main Post Offices.

Telexes are sometimes found where there's no phone. They usually rely on a friendly business or Government office.

Shortwave radio provides news on the BBC World Service etc.

TV may provide access to satellite world news (CNN, BBC).

Local media may provide fascinating views and information.

TWO-WAY

Telephones are increasingly available. Many towns have at least a telephone bureau and with the advent of satellites many of these now have direct dialling. Trunk lines are sometimes busy or crossed and patience is then needed. If signal delay and echoing make conversation difficult, don't interject with 'um' and 'ah' or interrupt (it confuses) and end alternating statements with the word, 'Over'.

Fax is phenomenal: it circumvents the post, is less liable to bad lines than phoning, doesn't depend on people being awake, yet can offer an immediate reply if they are and often conveys more, more cheaply than other systems. Where phone lines allow, it is spreading rapidly, not only replacing telexes, but cheap enough for many private lines.

Two-way radio is usually used to relay messages from remote areas up-country. Timing is pre-arranged. Some Missions use this, e.g. MAF. Governments may be unwilling to allow it.

Satellite uplinks are expensive, but necessary for some urgent or vital international communications, such as major relief programmes, or live media coverage. Some Governments are very reticent to grant permission for non-Consular uses.

e-mail requires a compatible computer, appropriate modem and address. Some countries prevent access to the WorldWideWeb; local access can take months to arrange. Direct communications to a bulletin board is another possiblity.

MEMOS

Note useful contacts below (including street and postal addresses if different):

CONTACT	PHONE	FAX	TELEX	ADDRESS
Name				

Home

Main

Back up

Organisers

Main

Back up

Overseas

Main

Back up

Others

FOREIGN NEWS

The BBC World Service provides home, international and your continent's news. More TV owners can now access CNN or BBC World TV. You might want to buy *News Week* or subscribe to a weekly news sheet such as *The Guardian Weekly*.

LOCAL NEWS

Local media provide variable quality, not least when heavily controlled. At worst, you will see a marvellously distorted world through Government eyes. At best, you will find telling, new perspectives challenging your assumptions.

THE HOME END

A note from the destination airport may be encouraging. Send a letter home with any returning contacts. You may all benefit more than expected, from regular contact. Be wary of increasing anxiety with pre-arranged phone times (unless the system is reliable, you're available, or you want someone to check your safety). If they phone you, then they won't assume you're dead, but will know if the line is busy or crossed!

CONTENT

Distance makes the imagination grow stronger! Innocent comments about illness, insects, accommodation, travel, money, incidents or feelings can all sow fear. Be real, but sensitive. If news is worrying, stress the final outcome, or request specific assistance. If you mention unresolved issues, arrange a follow-up communication.

UN-CONFIDENTIAL COMMUNICATIONS!

Some governments routinely open mail and tap phones, so don't comment on politics or sensitive issues. In Muslim and anti-Christian states, it is best for no one to refer to your Christian or Missionary nature, nor to mention local believers by name, nor to raise the subject of converts. In more extreme states, headed paper, Bible quotes or any hint of Christianity could mean trouble for local Christians, ministries and you.

PRAYER LETTER

This is invaluable on longer assignments. Make a (willing) address list and find your prayer secretary. Mail regularly, perhaps quarterly. Make them interesting, short, with facts, personal information and key prayer points. It might be widely read, occasionally by unwelcome readers, so be more careful than with personal letters.

Focus on your needs. Also send one before you leave and after returning.

JOURNAL

A journal is an excellent aide memoire.

REPORTS

Immerse yourself in it if required, to better integrate your experience. Maybe write an article for your church newsletter, local paper or university rag etc., though you will have to concentrate hard on style and readability.

MEMOS

Note radio frequencies and subscription contacts below:

STRESSORS

Any object, situation or thought can be a Stressor and the more of it, the stronger are its effects. It is a subjective perception; one person may react more than another to the same situation or notion.

Stress is the body's reaction to Stressors. Without any Stress, there is the potential for boredom. Optimum Stress can lead to the excitement of meeting a difficult but surmountable challenge.

SYMPTOMS

Too much Stress is called Strain and can lead to over-exhaustion (sometimes called 'burnout') and other symptoms. These can include fast breathing, a pounding heart, ringing in the ears, tingling fingertips and lips, headache, 'butterflies' in the tummy and nausea. There can be more visible things like shaking, diarrhoea, vomiting. Also more insidious things like not wanting to eat, sleep problems, nightmares, emotional swings, weight changes, anxiety, depression, personality changes and losing contact with reality.

Your underlying level of Stress will affect how much more you can take. It can be worsened by a whole range of life changes and experiences in the previous year or more.

COPING

- Have you coped under stress before? This is a good predictor (particularly similar or severe stress).
- Do you know much about yourself? Sometimes Stress makes personality traits more extreme. Knowing how you will probably react can make things easier when you do.
- Have you developed ways to deal with Stress positively, using active/creative hobbies or other ways of relaxing? If so, take some relevant paraphernalia with you. If not and there is time, try to develop a hobby. Or join someone overseas in theirs. Passive occupation is useful in dealing with stress for a short while, such as when waiting, but tends to promote escapism.
- Where everything that happens is unpredictable, stress will be increased. Know a bit about the climate, culture, language and food you will encounter, if possible. Such knowledge is like a vaccination against Stress.
- A reasonable level of physical fitness (and maintaining it) will help you cope better. If you are unwell or under the weather, this will reduce your ability to deal with additional pressures. Have a proper rest when ill.

- Make talking about feelings normal in all sorts of situations. Remember that depression, anger and fear are quite normal and usually not 'spiritual symptoms'.
- Make things easier for yourself if you need to: reduce your workload, stop perfectionism and allow compromise. Don't get up so early or go to bed so late, take time off (cancel meetings), *prioritise and cut radically*.
- If you have symptoms, seek professional advice.

MEMOS

Rate your current stress level and review it overseas: (Note recent stressors.)

Outline how you will cope with additional stress:

TYPICAL STRESS LEVELS

- My research at Tear Fund amongst Short Termers suggests that **two thirds feel overstressed to some degree**, during their project (three quarters of these because of it, the remainder because they started and remained overstressed). **The other third don't find the project adds extra stress**.
- Another perspective on these figures indicates that **half feel the project increases their stress and half don't**.
- The flip side of this is that **one in ten become bored** and **one quarter are overfatigued**. However, *hardly any feel their programme is a waste of time or are unable to cope*.

It is worthwhile being prepared for the possibility that you will find your project stressful. Graham Fawcett, a YWAM Psychologist says, 'Telling (Short-Termers) that they will feel bad is not a self-fulfilling prophecy but a protection.'[1]

ADJUSTMENT PHASES

Immersion in a new culture, climate and set of circumstances can be simplistically described with the following consecutive phases: *Honeymoon, Disorientation, Reaction, Adjustment, Integration* (this doesn't describe everybody). Overall stress level is likely to increase through the first three phases, before reducing again in the last two (and performance will correspondingly decrease before increasing: a 'U'-shaped curve). As with the grieving process, it is also possible to move around between phases:

Honeymoon. This phase lasts for a few months and most Short-Termers do not move much further than this. It is characterised by excitement, energy, flexibility, willing dependence on others and a flood of interesting experiences.

Disorientation follows as excitement wanes, new experiences become overwhelming, energy is drained away, cultural gaffes begin to embarrass you and you realise how little you can communicate or do for yourself.

Reaction can take a host of forms. These may include a selection from: withdrawal, homesickness, depression, superiority, inferiority, perfectionism, obsessions, hostility, risk-taking etc.

Adjustment is the positive face of reaction. Its marks include patience, determination, optimism, self-discipline, and a willingness to tolerate and learn through humiliation.

Integration. Few can regain the 'highs' of the Honeymoon phase. At last however, you will hopefully begin to settle and feel comfortable, with a palpable insight into the culture, language and people. Sometimes there is a moment of euphoria; a sudden realisation that you fit in.

CULTURE SHOCK

All this is normal, but strong or persistent Disorientation and Reaction is sometimes called 'Culture Shock' and you may need wise counsel. After one year, most people who don't get stuck find themselves somewhere in the last two phases.

MEMOS

Review your position occasionally, when overseas:

1 *Graham Fawcett*, 'A Psychological Perspective of Selection, Briefing and Debriefing' in: Proceedings of a Meeting of Christian Short Term Overseas Programme Organisers, Tear Fund, 1993, p.13–15.

BEGGING

In almost every city, you will face beggars. In 1990, a Tear Fund / Youth For Christ Team in India asked a woman begging what her name was. 'I think I had one once,' she answered. What did she want in life? 'A Mango . . . and then to die.' It's not all right, just because Jesus said there would always be poor among us! It should challenge our lifestyle, politics, economics, selfishness, theology, complacency. You can't change the world, but change yourself and begin to influence others. Talk to local Christians. Talk to beggars. This may educate you and remind them and you of their value. If you can't just walk on, give a small amount to only one beggar each time you see them. Or take a limited amount of change around with you and eke it out as opportunity arises.

POVERTY

Shanty towns are growing, as poor or displaced rural families migrate to cities in hope of work. Globally, three fifths of the world earn just over 5% of the world's income.[1] Christians are not exempt, despite the lies of the Prosperity movement. You may face requests for help, even from project staff, perhaps to pay for a child's treatment. Ask wise local Leaders what to do. Don't promise to send things back from home. Your money can't solve everything. Jesus himself withdrew from crowds needing healing. Also, it is acceptable in some cultures to ask acquaintances for financial assistance, particularly when they are plainly richer. It is then also very acceptable to politely say no.

STREET CHILDREN

Without contraception or the safety net we take for granted, many families can't provide for all their children. Others, whom we'd expect to end up in care as orphans or through abuse, have nowhere to go. Some are sold or kidnapped into slave labour or prostitution. They adapt their lifestyles for survival, often hounded by death squads, brothel owners and paedophiles. They may depend on begging, prostitution and crime. Don't be taken for a ride, or needlessly cause yet another broken heart on leaving. Most of them will be little adults, more worldly wise than you. The best assistance is to fund established programmes, or gain adequate training and experience before trying to help.

INJUSTICE

This is a crippling burden for anyone to face, let alone without legal assistance or resources to fall back on. Much of the world lives in fear of corrrupt authority and with good cause. If you do fight someone's corner, bear in mind possible reprisals once you leave. Ask a wise local Leader.

SUFFERING

Medical hardship is rife, but often hidden. Healthcare workers may be struck by poor standards and practice far out of their depth! Curative care may treat a few, but consider the need for community healthcare. Get yourself adequately trained first. Make yourself rest properly when there.

MEMOS

How do you approach these and other issues?

1 Human Development Report 1992, United Nations Development Pro-gramme, Oxford University Press, Oxford, 1992.

THEORETICAL INSIGHTS

Facing change, you won't suddenly discover an auxiliary personality! Personal insight is an invaluable coping tool; learning from previous reactions to similar circumstances is even better. There are many different ways to examine your personality. A useful one is the Myers-Briggs analysis. Its drawbacks include the descriptive names for personality traits which differ from natural meanings and its bias towards Western traits. Theoretical approaches offer opportunities for insight and ways to develop less preferred approaches, to achieve a balance. They also offer to predict potential behaviour.

EXPERIENTIAL LEARNING

The objective is to simulate conditions, review reactions and develop optimal approaches. An objective observer is essential. This forms much of the training for pilots, paramedics, the military, fire crews etc. Wycliffe run a simulation course, for would-be translators. Tear fund have piloted a major crisis simulation for Long Term workers and a frustratingly real airport simulation during most Short Term Team training. Role play is a less realistic, but valuable training format.

DETERMINANTS OF PERSONALITY

Supernatural influences, taken for granted in the Bible, are accorded a predominant influence in many cultures.

Congenital traits are ones we're born to develop. This notion flowed from classical determinism. The rise of genetics and studies of separated, identical twins etc. have offered it modern credentials and a recent renaissance.

Environmental influences have been seen as vital since Old Testament writers tied discipline to child development. The scientific community favoured this concept through most of this century, after psychoanalysts and researchers postulated the importance of early childhood experiences.

Gender is a sensitive issue, not least if Christians accuse each other of sexism or squeezing into the world's mould. Valid, useful generalisations can be made about sex differences, whether they are inherent, modelled by stereotypes or both: Deborah Tannen[1] argues that men tend to 'see themselves as individuals in a world of hierarchies.' Independence and failure are main themes for them. On the other hand, women often 'see themselves as individuals in a network of connections.' For them, community and intimacy are key.

Culture is viewed by some anthropologists as the main personality determinant. They point to different cultures taking opposite approaches, such as reversed gender roles and the moral superiority of community versus independence. This will be explored further in the chapter on cross-cultural expectations.

MEMOS

What do you know about yourself and how have you reacted to stress before?

1 *Deborah Tannen*, You Just Don't Understand—Men And Women In Conversation, Virago, 1991.

The Team Dynamic is like an independent yet intangible personality. A Team is valuable, because it potentially has synergy: the sum achievable is greater than just the addition of individual efforts. Its Achille's heel is more its potential conflict resolution skills than its component individuals.

INDIVIDUAL TEAM ROLES

Belbin[1] has usefully measured individuals' preferred Team roles. These personality characteristics may only emerge when in a Team and may differ from expectations. Paraphrased, Belbin's eight roles include:

1. A person who concentrates on doing the job.
2. A co-ordinator and controller.
3. An achiever, prioritising and pushing the Team onward.
4. An original thinker; the key 'ideas' person.
5. A lateral thinker who can usually see ways out of crises.
6. An auditor, pointing out mistaken notions.
7. An encourager, enhancing others' roles.
8. Someone keen to ensure the task is finished carefully.

TEAM INTERACTIONS

Some interesting Team traits have been noted by observers:

Authority reactions can be bizarre: Leaders are sometimes ostracised, unfairly criticised, arbitrarily disagreed with and occasionally followed blindly. A disproportionate loss of confidence may follow a minor failing. All this can be heightened for a Leader emerging within a leaderless group.

Scapegoating occurs, where the most individual member is targeted with the group's misplaced frustrations.

Groupthink is a phenomenon whereby the Team agree to a course of action which is more extreme than the average opinion (rarely, even more so than its most extreme one).

Inertia applies to the difficulty with which a Team agrees on change. It promotes stability (and security, which many Teams will strive for) but damages adaptability.

Shame is toward a community, what guilt is toward authority. It arises from behaviour or thought identified as being outside group norms. It can arise from intolerance, stifled debate, lack of compromise (and sometimes sin). It may relate to any issue including gender roles, spiritual topics, physical symptoms, behaviour, etc.

Displacement reactions are the inappropriate venting of a shameful emotion e.g. the Team member who criticises their colleagues' greed, may actually be 'homesick', or 'guilty about yesterday's beggar', etc.

TEAM DEVELOPMENT

Four progressive stages have been distinguished.[2] Some pre-departure meeting, phoning and writing, is invaluable:

1. *Forming*. At this stage, members become acquainted.
2. *Norming*. Participants now begin to 'let their hair down'. Preliminary norms and taboos are formed.
3. *Storming*. The group engages with differences, and attempts are made to negotiate with norms and taboos.
4. *Performing*. Hopefully, the group will now know its strengths and limits and operate to maximum efficiency.

MEMOS

What roles do you think you prefer?

What about other Team members?

Occasionally review Team dynamics:

1 *R. Meredith Belbin*, Management Teams—Why They Succeed or Fail, 1981, Butterworth/Heinemann, Oxford.
2 B. W. Tuckman (1965), quoted in J. F. Benson, Working More Creatively in Groups, 1987, Tavistock Publications, London, p. 79.

WITH THE TEAM

Many Short-Termers depend on each other, without family, friends or culture. Try to get on with everybody. There is little escape from conflict, particularly in a small Team. Resolve problems quickly.

EXCLUSIVE FRIENDSHIPS

Returnees often mention disharmony within a Team, because of exclusive (same or opposite sex) relationships. This may be appropriate, or actually (or interpreted as) a retreat into isolated security, aloofness; a snub at authority and a withdrawal from availability (physical or supportive).

PHYSICAL RELATIONSHIPS

There are few non-Western cultures, where visible physical expressions of friendship between members of the opposite sex are acceptable (holding hands, touching, hugging or kissing). Some cultures consider an unmarried couple together alone, even in a lift, to be amoral. Westerners are frequently perturbed by seeing men holding hands.

WITH NATIONALS

Your best passport to understanding the local culture, is a friendship with a National. Beware incipient nationalism or cultural superiority. There will often be misconceptions on both sides. Legacies of colonialism and imperialism still remain in places and sometimes this will work against you. Also, as a foreigner you are easily capable of causing offence. Sometimes your failings may tactfully not be pointed out (you are after all, a guest). If you sensitively ask National friends about ways you could clash less with their culture, you may be surprised what comes out. They may also respect you more for having asked.

WITH OTHER EXPATRIATES

A number of Short-Termers find another Missionary the hardest person to get along with. For Teams, as well as the occasional difficult resident supervisor, para-Team members are sometimes the problem. These are people who tag onto the Team for some or all of their time, from a different source. They can cause serious disruption and thus resentment. Wise treatment is sometimes circumspect treatment.

CONFLICT RESOLUTION

1. Beware your personality's extremes, amplified by stress.
2. Debate when calmer, with a referee(!) if necessary.

3. Be open, real and honest about your feelings.
4. Love (1 Corinthians 13).
5. Give in if possible (Philippians 2:1–11).
6. Don't judge or pursue your point unrelentingly (Romans 14).
7. Without anger, there are *few essential issues.*
8. The World should see you are Christians by your love.

(Rhena Taylor[1] gives further insights.)

MEMOS

Outline key issues for your Team, within your local overseas context and review overseas:

1 *Rhena Taylor*, The Prisoner And Other Stories, 1987, MARC Europe, Watford.

A new culture may offer significant challenges to our norms, if we can overrule our prejudices. Seeing through merely cultural differences, to actual moral questions, can be very confusing and we are apt to be judgmental. Geert Hofstede has studied cultural differences in management,[1] shedding light on organisational structure, leadership styles and motivation. His terms are underlined below. (His book should be referred to regarding individual countries):

THE CULTURAL CONCEPT

At the root of culture are **values** we are imbued with from birth, often unrealised and held as self evident truths. These are hard to discover as they may be taken for granted, undefined or expected to be inherent to foreigners also.

These values are expressed through **rituals**, personified by **heroes** and represented in **symbols**. A foreigner will impact these visible signs, which may not reveal the values. They may well conflict with his or her own cultural values. Hence the confusion, condescension or disdain of some observers.

VALUES

Most cultures ascribe inherent value to aspects of:

1. Power Distance—the acceptability of power being vested in dominant authorities and figureheads.
2. Individualism/Collectivism—the importance of submitting to a community's interests, rather than your own.
3. Masculinity/Femininity—the necessity for defined roles.
4. Uncertainty Avoidance—the desire to define and predict.
5. Long/Short Term Orientation (identified by Chinese studies)—the desirability of stability versus change.

VISIBLE SIGNS

Offence is caused in the visible arena, because few rituals obviously follow on from an understanding of relevant core values. Observers have frequently noted key areas where offence can be given by Westerners, including:

Inadequate greetings	Being time bound
Not honouring age	Self-centredness
Presumptuousness of youth	Eurocentric notions
Inhospitableness	Requiring appointments
Women's roles	Male/female interactions
Liberal dressing code	Social use of left hand
Public criticism/contradiction	'Taking the mickey'

The corollary is that some Westerners criticise the opposite of the above and also, the issues below:

Not queueing	Bias to family/friends
Hygiene/cleanliness	Decor/maintenance
Using 'Fat' as a compliment	Attitudes to privacy

CONCLUSION

Don't believe that you are the only one adapting to a new culture. The warm acceptance of locals sometimes suggests an even greater adaptability on their part, when we later discover our various faux pas!

MEMOS

What are your cultural values?

What will local values overseas be?

What are key, visible signs of local culture?

Are there wrong things at home or in the local context, justified as culturally necessary?

1 *Geert Hofstede*, Cultures And Consequences—Software Of The Mind, 1991, McGraw Hill.

PREPARATION

Prayer
Pray regularly with someone (prayer partners or triplets) before you leave and keep them praying for you.

Attitudes
Examine yours to people with differing Christian backgrounds. Know what you believe and why but be receptive. However, you should resolve conflicts by your humility. Problem issues:

- **Exercising spiritual gifts**. Some are suspicious if you suggest these are from God. Others would rather break fellowship than deny God an opportunity to speak.
- **Worship styles**. Some think quiet, reflective worship coupled with a disdain for loud choruses, denies God his praise. The former may think that the latter are just getting emotionally 'high' and ignoring their minds.
- **Spiritual Warfare**. Some think that 'personified' evil spirits are at best allegories; at worst they are ascribed far too much power. Others think that the 'powers of darkness' are key enemies, often even in the guise of 'psychological' or 'medical' problems.
- **Compromise**. A dirty word to some; they consider that every doubt or question reveals a hidden anti-Christ. Others see broken fellowship as a last resort, following firm denial of a small number of essential beliefs.

Presentations
Prepare a two-minute outline of your testimony to Jesus in your life. A sermon or two, plus one or two wordless drama sketches are also invaluable: In church, you or the Team may often face a request to share or give a sermon at short notice. Know also, how to pass on your faith.

Reading
Read a good book before going, take another to read and leave one there. Remember your Bible and study materials.

PRACTICE

Devotions
Don't allow personal time with God to disappear. In a Team, there is also tremendous value in group devotion. But beware of getting overtired with too early or late sessions.

Local Christians
Try to listen to and learn from local Christians. Ask them questions. Some seasoned overseas travellers are unwilling to preach on one-off

visits, since they will be much less keyed in to the local culture and congregation.

Outward signs
In many cultures, there isn't the squeamishness we face in the West, talking about religion. You may find people wanting to chat with you about everything including your beliefs. In some cultures, patients might be surprised if doctors don't pray to their God as they set about healing!

OVERSPIRITUALISING

You may well face an emotional roller-coaster from start to finish, just because of stress. Don't believe everything is a major spiritual issue. When you are less tired, eating familiar food and unstressed, things may return to 'normal'.

MEMOS

Outline key spiritual objectives before leaving:

Outline your testimony:

Review objectives and other lessons learnt:

SOURCES OF FUNDS

It is good to have at least two sources of 'hard' currency (US$, UK£, DM etc.), as cash, travellers cheques, credit cards, Cirrus or a cash card, a transfer facility (arranged from your bank to a local one or FOREX bureau), a 'wiring' service etc. If staying for long, try to get a local foreign currency bank account. Local currency is often unobtainable outside the country and must be bought after arrival. Keep separately a record of unused travellers cheque numbers.

EXCHANGE RATES

Regulations are occasionally in force, with exchange only allowed through authorised channels, not the 'black market'. At the airport, change only what is needed, since exchange rates may be worse than in town. In countries with rampant inflation, you may do well to exchange a little every day or week, because it devalues so quickly; otherwise pay for services in 'hard' currency, if this isn't illegal.

IMPORTING AND EXPORTING CURRENCY

Some countries require you to declare all your 'hard' currency on arrival and to keep official receipts for all exchanges. On departure, they may check for a discrepancy and fine you, detain you or confiscate unexplained cash. Some countries won't let you buy back 'hard' currency at the end; others won't let you take any of their currency out. If this is the case, don't rip up spare cash in anger: this has landed people in trouble.

EXCHANGE FACILITIES

Sometimes outside major cities, there is nowhere even to cash US$ travellers cheques, let alone use a credit card. Almost everywhere though, someone will be willing to exchange US$ cash, particularly low denomination notes. Check with a travel agent for local details, or a specialist travel guide book e.g. the Lonely Planet series.

LOCAL CURRENCY

These are now almost all based on decimal notation. Countries with an appalling record of inflation may hand you vast quantities of notes in exchange; a stuffed envelope for £5, a suitcase for £100!

PERSONAL SPENDING AND TAXIS

Buying like tourists and staying where they stay, will cost you nearly the same as in Europe. Remember this, if you anticipate going on safari or a guided jungle trek. In markets, **bartering** is often a way of life and can be fun. Don't get fleeced! If worried, get a local to barter for you. Remember no matter how much of a bargain you think you've got, sellers won't barter away their margin! If buying something cheap, have low denomination cash; don't accept 'no change' arguments. With taxis, agree a fixed price before driving away, or if it has a meter, ensure it is 'working' before you set off.

MEMOS

Write locally relevant notes for each section, below:

You may ask, why bother? Is it really necessary? Isn't English the most widely spoken language in the world? Will I ever use the new language again? Some may want to give up before starting (myself included) saying, 'I'm no good at languages.' Have a go.

NEEDS

If you are planning to live or travel in a non-English speaking country for more than a few weeks without translation assistance, there is no way you will assimilate into the local culture without language and it will only worsen your disorientation.

A Team without translators might almost as well not be there. It is wise for a Team to have at least two members speaking the language, for those countries where French, Spanish or Portuguese are widely known. For others, you will need translation, even if you have to pay for it.

ADVANTAGES

– Learning some of a language can be a useful introduction to the culture, people and their history.
– Willingness to attempt to communicate in an unfamiliar language can break down barriers and prejudices.
– You will be less isolated, with less of a tendency to retreat into familiar Team or expatriate ghettos.
– It can be a tool to develop friendships with locals.
– Learning and practising whilst new to the country will provide your excuse for making mistakes. Less allowance might be granted after a long time without progress.

PREPARATION

– At the very least, try to find a relevant phrase book to take with you.
– Try to find a study guide, to learn some of the language structure and vocabulary. You will need to allow time.
– If you can locate (and afford) a cassette guide, you may find this easier, since you will be able to practice useful phrases and correct pronunciation.
– Find someone who speaks the language, to practice your pronunciation on and pick up tips from. They may even be willing to teach you a little.
– If you have the time and money, enrol in a night class well before your trip. This will provide a disciplined learning process, with added motivation and support of class mates. Practice opportunities

and skilled correction, as well as tailored learning, make this ideal.

OVERSEAS

If you have the time, you may well find someone local very happy to give you more structured lessons for free. Language teachers may be much cheaper than at home.

TEFL/TESL (Teaching English as a Foreign/Second Language)

To teach overseas, do a one month intensive TEFL certificate course; TESL to teach visitors/immigrants to the UK.

MEMOS

Outline needs and review progress:

THE PROJECT

Hopefully, the programme Organiser will provide you with enough information about the project you will be going to. Their previous involvement or the history of the contact would be helpful. It may also be worth writing to introduce yourself, but take the Organiser's advice first about who should and when. Talking to someone who has been before is useful, especially if they have slides. You may want to know about the people you'll meet, the local environment, accommodation, washing and toilet facilities. Also, food and cooking, the local culture, behavioural and safety hints, recreational facilities, transport conditions, costs and standards of living, clothing and bedding needs and mosquito net requirements. Knowing the electrical voltage and plug type may be useful.

THE TASK

Many Returners say that one of their few frustrations was not knowing enough about what they would be doing, or it being different upon arrival. Long-Termers too, are often frustrated by delays, changes to plans, cross-cultural misunderstandings, problems with bureaucracy, long distance communication, civil unrest and logistics. These are facts of life through most of the world. It is no wonder that Short-Termers frequently find their project plagued by one or a number of these problems, with no time to resolve them satisfactorily before departure. Hence the sudden changes to half-baked, on-the-spot or back-up plans. Just be prepared and make the best of them; it's a valuable learning experience.

THE COUNTRY

You should read up about the country you will be visiting. Find out about the climate, customs, language, food, travel facilities, history, topography, religious and natural history. I recommend the Lonely Planet series, found in most book shops. They are less up-beat than some of the others, such as the Insight Guides, which tend to gloss over problems you might face. The Rough Guides are invaluable if travel and accommodation will be key parts of your trip. If you had the space and the least inclination, I would recommend binoculars and a copy of the relevant Collin's Guide to birds, there being such a profusion in the tropics. Operation World[1] will provide valuable religious insights into your destination as well.

TRAVEL ADVICE

I have not yet read a better book, if you wish to travel fairly independently or extensively, than The Traveller's Handbook[2]—nearly

600 pages of advice and 300 of useful facts and addresses, including sources of detailed maps.

TRAVEL PLANS

If you are making all your own plans, refer to later sections in the book for *Organisers* and *Leaders*.

MEMOS

Write locally relevant notes for each section, below, and continued on the memo sheets at the end of the book:

1 *Patrick Johnstone*, Operation World, 1994, OM Publishing, Carlisle.
2 The Traveller's Handbook, 1994, WEXAS, London.

THE AIRPORT

Imagine a jet disgorging 300 passengers, an hour before sunset, onto a baking, cracked tarmac apron. You're sweating from waiting an hour on the plane. You should have landed this morning (or last Thursday if it wasn't overbooked) but they decided to fly to the second stop first and come back later. Arrivals turns out to be a small room with a single, slowly rotating ceiling fan. You are perhaps obliged to change US$100 at a cash desk before proceeding. You've lost your immunisation certificates and only amusement after you offer to show the injection site, gets you through. Then to passport control where, after thirty minutes, you are told you should have filled in a disembarkation card on the plane. You take one and go to the back of the queue. Eventually, a new officer speaks to you in rapid non-English. After gesticulation, a phrase book and translation from a fellow passenger, you realise he wants to know your accommodation street address, not the postal address. After this, a civilian takes your passport out of your hand, and walks off into a quiet corner. He looks at your visa, then tells you the entry date stamped is tomorrow's. He suggests a US$50 'arrangement fee'. You extract yourself from this. At the baggage collection, one bag has disappeared and another is torn open. You make your way past a couple of wooden slatted benches to face an armed soldier blocking your exit. You return to the 'Customs' benches to have a purple chalk cross marked on your bag. The soldier lets you through, but another civilian wants to check your passport. He lets you go after surreptitious eye contact with your former accuser. The airline desk is closed because it's dark, so now you can't report the loss or damage. There are, however, a hundred shouting, mauling people around you, some apparently taxi drivers or their agents trying to drag you, attached to your bag, to their car. No one is here to meet you. Eventually you select one, only to find the meter 'broken' and you're arguing over the fare. After the airport (not usually so bad), the rest is a dream, unless in trouble, needing a visa or a work permit!

VISAS AND WORK PERMITS

In some countries, you must register your presence with the local police or immigration department after a limited period. In most, you must keep your passport with you at all times. Renewing your visa within the country may be possible, sometimes only once, for a limited period. Occasionally, renewals may be made at the border, crossing back from a neighbouring country. Work permits are usually obtained in-country and after many months, if at all.

AUTHORITIES

The Police and Military often seem overwhelming, usually with guns and sometimes roadblocks. Be polite and don't offer a bribe. Some countries have Tourist Police to protect gullible foreigners. Use these in preference. Understand that extortion (a threat) is not bribery (a request) and the former is much less likely from Authorities.

MEMOS

Ask a non-EC resident student, immigrant or refugee about their experiences trying to enter the UK.

Note examples of bureaucracy you meet.

DRIVING LICENCES

Your own licence may be valid for a short period or needed to obtain a local licence. An International Driving Permit is usually required outside the EC. Some countries may require you to take a local driving test after a few months. Further details and the permit, can be obtained from the AA.

CARNET DE PASSAGE

Needed to drive a vehicle through many countries outside the EC, it will require a deposit or security, up to the new replacement value of the car and import dues (sometimes over 150%). Talk to the AA about this possible need, if you are taking any vehicle.

VEHICLE INSURANCE

Personal liability clauses in many travel policies exclude third party injury liability if driving. The cost of hospital care for a person injured may be phenomenal, let alone legal costs in defending yourself. A local policy may not be worth anything, though more are being underwritten by respectable agents such as Lloyds and may be worth more. You may find a policy before leaving. Contact the AA or RAC for advice. Either way, small print for 'Third World' policies can exclude unmetalled roads!

THE ACCIDENT

As a foreigner, you may automatically be blamed, despite having been stationary! You may even be arrested, fined on the spot or requested to 'make some arrangement' (a bribe) with the police or military. Sometimes, it is best to settle a compensation fee with the other driver, to save complications. Get names and addresses of several witnesses if possible. If hostility develops, it may be wise to drive off and place yourself immediately under the care of the police of military. Do not just disappear. If someone is injured, you may feel morally obliged to get them to hospital. If insured, try to talk to the insurer, before paying for more than urgent transport and immediate medical care. Expect unimaginable hassle, though it won't always materialise.

AVOIDING PROBLEMS

It's best to use a local driver in a safe local vehicle, in daylight; perhaps the local project has a car and driver. Taxis are often cheaper than in the UK and can sometimes be hired all day or for long distances.

ROADSIDE ASSISTANCE

There are places where this exists! In Europe, national organisations co-operate. Talk to the AA/RAC before leaving.

KNOWLEDGEABLE DRIVING

If you must drive, I recommend buying 'The Traveller's Handbook',[1] with a wealth of tips—from shipping a vehicle to driving in sand. It has a country by country list of licence and import regulations.

MEMOS

Write locally relevant notes for each section, below:

1 The Traveller's Handbook, 1994, WEXAS, London.

WAITING

Waiting can be a major pastime. Carry a juicy novel and/or travel games with you, when travelling or dealing with officialdom. A hobby can relieve stress and bring enjoyment. Taking leisure time will increase your work efficiency.

PHOTOGRAPHY

If photos are just for cherished memories, prints taken however you like will do. For slides, you'll need more effort. Beware dull holiday snaps! Protect your camera, since you can expect more extreme conditions. Keep your film in a sealed plastic bag in the fridge if it's hot and take as much as you can as well as spare batteries; they can be expensive or difficult to buy. Find a friend, book or magazine, for advice on cameras, composing shots and giving slide shows. At airports, I haven't yet found a sympathetic operator to hand search my film, rather than force it under the X-ray. Don't put photographic equipment in hold baggage or it may be broken or stolen. For safety, avoid photographs of the military, police, official cars, airports, aircraft, bridges, government buildings, civil disturbance, public punishments, or coup situations. Also, integrity demands that you seek permission to take anyone's photograph, not least if displaying poverty, suffering, reduced dignity or your own voyeurism. Ask a wise local for specific advice.

OTHER HOBBIES

– If you *paint or sketch*, you will probably need to take everything with you. It can be very rewarding.
– If a *collector*, there may be restrictions. Some countries don't allow removal of animals, religious figurines, ceremonial items, archaeological objects, coral, etc.
– *Nature observers* will often be astounded at the variety of butterflies, birds, etc. Be careful using binoculars in sensitive situations (see photography).
– *Snorkelling and SCUBA diving* may reveal a fantastic world. Rubber-soled shoes or full-sole fins are a must on tropical reefs, to avoid injury. Don't risk your life SCUBA diving without full training, except in shallow, one-one settings with a qualified instructor with a spare mouthpiece, knowing what all your equipment does and understanding underwater hand signals.
– *Safaris, mountain treks and boat journeys* can be immensely rewarding, usually expensive, requiring guides and sometimes porters. Use reputable operators. Have appropriate fitness, food, footwear, first aid, filters (etc. for water); clothing, climbing,

cooking and survival equipment; bedding, insect protection and maps. Think about taking some of these with you overseas.

– If *travelling*, consider flying internally, as it is quicker, safer and often cheaper than you'd think. Overland reality is often: top-heavy, unsafe vehicles, driven badly on pot-holed roads beside frightening gorges; cramped, toiletless, sweaty, with unclean food and water; on age-long journeys with frequent stops and break-downs.

MEMOS

Write a checklist of relevant paraphernalia to take:

Undoubtedly, your destination country will have a different religious history from your own. It is most likely that you will encounter an unfamiliar range of religious expression, despite living in a multi-cultural society at home. Operation World[1] provides up to date statistics on the religious make up of every region and country in the world. The Lion Handbook to the World's Religions[2] provides useful background relating to the main features of many religions.

REGIONAL RELIGIOUS MIXES

Based on Operation World figures.

Religion	Africa	Asia	Carib.	Eurasia[3]	Europe	Lat.Am.	Mid.East
Christian[a]	57%<	8%<	78%	51%<	78%	94%<	5%<
Islam	27%<	18%	1%	18%<	3%<		93%<
Hinduism		24%	2%				
Buddhism[b]		21%					
Primal	15%	2%	8%			2%<	1%
Others[c]	1%	2%	1%	2%	1%	1%	1%
None		25%	10%	29%	18%<	3%<	

%: Rounded to nearest unit; <: recent growth
[a]Protestants, Catholics, Orthodox, Sects and nominals
[b]Including Taoism and Shintoism
[c]Including main categories with less than 0.5%

ISLAM

Believers base their lives on: the Qur'an (believing it to be God's last revelation); the *Sunnah* (example of Muhammad's life in the Sira—biographies and Hadith—sayings); the *Sharia* (or legal principles); authoritative *interpretation* (based on sect); *tradition* and *culture*. The 'Four Pillars'—*Salat* (prayer); *Sawm* (fasting in Ramadan), *Zakat* (mandatory charity) and *Hajj* (pilgrimage to Mecca)—flow from the crucial *Tawheed*: 'There is no god but Allah.'[4]

HINDUISM

This is a *culture* and a way of life, rooted in *India*'s history. It is practised in a multitude of forms with a range of gods and beliefs. The *Ganges river* is revered, representing the water of life. *Reincarnation* as a higher life-form (and perhaps release after a near-perfect life) depends on *Karma* (good works and consequences in this life).

BUDDHISM, TAOISM, SHINTOISM

Gautama, the *Buddha*, taught his followers to attain *Nirvana* (enlightenment to a new reality) through *meditation* and *Karma* (see

Hinduism). This philosophy is now a religion by the addition of worship (Buddha and ancestors), customs and rites.

PRIMAL OR TRADITIONAL RELIGIONS

These are beliefs in a *spirit world*, affecting the visible world. Spirits from ancestors, animals, trees, earth, water, etc., *'possess'* visible objects or act independently. *'Medicine men'* are able to use or divert their powers. These beliefs overlay many main religions' *'folk'* *adherents*.

MEMOS

Make notes on the religious make-up of your destination, plus useful information. Update this with personal observations:

1 *Patrick Johnstone*, Operation World, 1994, OM Publishing, Carlisle.
2 A Lion Handbook—The World's Religions, 1982, Lion Publishing, Tring.
3 This is the name sometimes given to an area extending from the Ukraine into Central Asia.
4 *Ziauddin Sardar and Zafar Abbas Malik*, Muhammad For Beginners, 1994, Icon Books, Cambridge.

WHERE

Only God can say exactly how many Christians there are in the world, not least those who love and obey Jesus and accept the Bible as God's revelation. There are increasingly reliable statistics now available.[1] We have become used to thinking of the West as where most of the Evangelical Christians are. It is true that Evangelical growth in the West has outstripped population growth through the latter half of this century. However, growth rates outside the West have been faster since the early '60s. Numbers were about equal in the late '70s but are now estimated to be about three times greater outside than inside the West.

GROWTH

Ken Okeke[2] notes that early growth was through transplanted 'mainline' Western denominations such as Anglicans, Methodists, Baptists and Presbyterians. The recent phenomenal growth has mostly come through the development of what he calls 'Evango-Pentecostal Indigenous' churches (local denominations, under local leadership, with local priorities and local cultural assimilation): Operation World suggests that as a percentage of world wide Evangelicals, Pentecostals grew from 14% to 31% between 1960 and 1990.

NUMBERS

Overall, perhaps 5–6% of the world are Evangelical Christians, though almost a third of the world would consider themselves part of the Christian church in the widest sense. Clearly, we in the West who see the fruits of domestic Mission are not seeing anything like the church growth in much of the rest of the world:

REGIONAL EVANGELICAL STATISTICS

From Operation World figures.

Region	Africa	Asia	Carib.	Eurasia	Europe	Lat.Am.	Mid.East
Pop.[a]	0.56B	3.21B	0.04B	0.29B	0.51B	0.46B	0.38B
Ev.[b]	13.2%	3.1%	11.1%	0.9%	2.8%	11.1%	0.4%
Ev.G.R.[c]	7.0%	7.0%	5.1%	7.7%	1.6%	8.8%	7.2%
Pop.G.R.	3.0%	1.8%	1.4%	0.7%	0.3%	2.0%	2.7%
Mission[d]	3.7K	9.6K	<0.1K	<0.1K	15.8K	2.1K	<0.1K

[a]Population (Billions); [b]Evangelicals; [c]Growth Rate; [d]Locals going as cross-cultural Missionaries (Thousands).

The table above indicates the following:

1. There are more Evangelicals in Asia than any other single region (including North America).
2. Huge numbers are becoming Evangelical Christians in Africa, Asia (half of these in China) and Latin America.
3. In every region, Evangelical growth rate is faster than the population growth rate, mostly by two to five times.
4. There are around 15,500 non-Western Long Term Missionaries working outside their own cultures, compared to around 60,000 Western cross-cultural Long-Termers, including North Americans not shown in the table.

MEMOS

Make notes on the Christian make-up of your destination, plus useful information. Update this with personal observations:

1 *Patrick Johnstone*, Operation World, 1994, OM Publishing, Carlisle.
2 *Ken Okeke*, 'Understanding The National Church' in: Prepared To Serve, ed. Derek Williams, 1989, Tear Fund, London, p.65–73.

CHECK-IN

Airport paranoia reigns. Relevant questions may be asked by security or check-in staff. As well as avoiding banned items (see your ticket for a list), heed the following:

1. Pack your own bags and then keep them in sight, (to prevent theft or anyone slipping a package in).
2. Don't carry items for strangers, even to 'help'.
3. Don't carry sealed packages for friends (seal them later), as it may concern security or customs officers.

If a passenger doesn't board the aircraft containing their luggage, the plane won't leave till this has been located and unloaded. Also, if the aircraft is delayed overnight after check-in, no one will then be allowed their luggage back before take-off.

SMUGGLING

Smugglers use various tactics, including: swapping your luggage; hiding items in your bag; asking you to help carry 'all my bags'; asking you to deliver a sealed package, etc. Anyone could be a smuggler. They will usually go through ahead of you, or pass your description to an accomplice.

BAGGAGE

Valuable items are best carried in hand luggage. Hold luggage is out of sight and a sturdy, locked container will look enticing! (Thieves aren't pressed for time: baggage frequently 'gets lost' or 'accidentally damaged', making a useful smoke-screen.) Avoid putting breakables in the hold.

THEFT

Don't leave valuables unsecured. In slow traffic, don't hang arms with jewellery or a watch out of a window. Keep cameras and handbags out of reach and lock doors and the boot. When walking, particularly in urban areas: ask about safety; don't dress like a tourist; don't go alone; carry little money; keep cameras unobtrusive. Reporting any incident to the police and receiving a receipt of report, is the only way you will claim anything back from the insurance company.

STRANGERS

You shouldn't owe any favours or encourage anyone wanting to 'help' you. Persistence can occasionally lead to aggression, particularly if offering unwanted or lewd services. Strangers have drugged drink or food bought for an unsuspecting traveller, before robbing them.

WOMEN

Women alone are easy prey: carry an alarm, particularly in a city; don't get in the front seat of a taxi; be wary of unknown taxis at night. (A friendly establishment or hotel may know a driver they can recommend and call for you.)

MUGGING

Don't offer resistance, delay or abuse. If you have split your money (e.g. money belt, wallet or purse), you may get away with offering only one of these, but don't risk your own or anyone else's safety.

MEMOS

Note local precautions as you pick them up:

FIGHTING

General: Obtain permission and follow instructions from the local Control (it may not be the Government). However, Government reprisals may follow you working outside their areas. The BBC World Service gives updates on local emergencies and carries Foreign Office advice. Talk to trusted local Leaders, particularly if in partnership. The British Government can appear over cautious, though not taking their advice may remove their responsibility. Make evacuation plans before a crisis. Short-Termers with little local knowledge or input can be a liability in emergencies. Don't endanger others if you feel called into danger.

Practical advice includes (though local situations vary):

– Have evacuation plans with contingencies for failure of each phase. Check feasibility with practice drills. Agree decision making authority and communication lines.
– Stop at armed challenges/roadblocks; don't resist threats.
– Cover and avoid glass if there might be shooting or explosions; lie flat, face down in a windowless room, corridor or cellar without external walls if shooting or explosions are occurring, to avoid crossfire and shrapnel.
– Register with British government and local authorities if entering a potentially dangerous area.
– Maintain regular external communication.

HOSTAGE SITUATIONS

Background: Evangelical Missionary Alliance members have an agreed approach. Essentially, they will not pay a ransom nor be part of political bargaining to obtain release. They will be prepared to negotiate otherwise. This is to prevent Missionaries from becoming known as an easy source of income, since they are often in remote, exposed areas.

The *following advice* may be useful: (Read Taken On Trust[1]).

– Only resist capture if you can easily escape (and want to), otherwise obey demands; ingratiating yourself to captors may make future violence against you harder.
– Answer interrogation honestly but if you will endanger others then consider whether you can passively withstand.
– Maintain hygiene: Physically separate toileting and food; wash hands and/or keep hand functions separate.

- Maintain fitness; eat; bring medical problems to your captors' attention since they will not want to lose you.
- Lie flat or follow instructions in rescue attempts—which usually happen unexpectedly.
- Beware 'Stockholm Syndrome'—emotional support by or for your captors—don't forget: **if they really cared, they wouldn't keep you hostage.**

SURVIVAL SCENARIOS

Remember: **Protection, Location, Water, and Food** (including First Aid, Shelter, Fire and Rescue).[2] If you are going to sea, trekking or boating, in remote forest, crossing desert, climbing mountains or in snow bound conditions, you should make adequate preparations. The Traveller's Handbook[3] gives some tips, but more specialist texts and training may be needed.

MEMOS

If you need an escape plan, write a copy here (remember contingencies) and continue it on the memo sheets at the end of the book:

1 *Terry Waite*, Taken On Trust, 1993, Hodder and Stoughton, London.
2 *John Wiseman*, SAS Survival Guide, 1993, Collins, Gem (HarperCollins), Glasgow.
3 The Traveller's Handbook, 1994, WEXAS, London.

INTRODUCTION

The Medical section is not intended to provide comprehensive travel medical advice. Buy, read and carry a useful guide such as Healthy Beyond Heathrow.[1] However, this section is intended to raise your awareness about most of the key issues, so that you understand the importance of knowing a bit more.

MEDICAL CHECK-UP

If you have a history of medical problems, are older, or going overseas for more than a few months, it would be worth having a medical. Interhealth or Care for Mission can provide advice. Interhealth can also review a Short-Termer's medical status, using questionnaires for you and your GP.

MALARIA

This is the most dangerous common disease you are likely to get in the tropics. More returning UK travellers die of malaria than of any other bacterial or parasitic infection. Throughout the tropics, it kills around 1 million children per year. It is caused by a tiny parasite called *Plasmodium* (with four species, the worst or 'malignant' one being *P. falciparum*). These live in human blood and liver cells and are spread round by female *Anopheles* mosquitoes feeding on human blood, mostly at dusk or at night. Different mosquito species prefer indoor or outdoor locations. *To prevent malaria:*

– Take correct anti-malarials (use a Travel Clinic). *You are stupid to take amateur advice from other travellers.*
– Seek medical advice urgently for any fever and flu symptoms, overseas and for up to a year after returning. *NB* **There are other viral and bacterial tropical fevers (insect, water, animal or blood borne), in some areas.**
– Avoid bites at dusk or night, using mosquito nets, repellants, sleeves, mosquito coils (contact Interhealth).

DIARRHOEA AND VOMITING

It is usually self-limiting, just needing bed rest and constant fluid intake, perhaps with Oral Rehydration Solution. Don't take 'gut-blockers' unless you need the convenience of a toilet-free journey or meeting. They don't treat the infection, but bottle it up! Also, there is usually no need for antibiotics unless prescribed by a reliable professional. (Don't be tempted to self-treat with potentially dangerous products from unregulated pharmacies). *Prevent it by:*

- Carefully selecting, cleaning or cooking food.
- Drinking (and toothbrushing with) safe water and fluids.
- Prevent deterioration by not working if ill.

(See the comprehensive guide in Healthy Beyond Heathrow.)

SEEK MEDICAL HELP IF
- There is marked tummy pain.
- Blood in the diarrhoea or vomit.
- Symptoms last 10 days or more.
- Vomiting prevents adequate drinking or the patient looks unwell; feverish; dry; minimal urine output; unconscious.

MEMOS
Note nearest safe emergency treatment centre:

Note emergency medical insurance contact procedure:

Note UK medical advisors' contact:

Note the additional medical information you will take overseas:

Note your anti-malarial advice:

Note relevant advice on food and drink precautions and plan how you will respond to potentially unsafe hospitality:

1 *Ted Lankester*, Healthy Beyond Heathrow, Revised Edition 1994, Inter-health, London.

AIDS

This stands for Acquired Immune Deficiency Syndrome. It is the name for a whole range of infections and illnesses, which usually only happen to people infected with HIV (the Human Immunodeficiency Virus). This is a virus which grows in white blood cells which are supposed to fight other infections. Eventually, these cells just can't do their job. Millions of people around the world are infected and millions more are affected as carers or orphans of people with HIV disease. After infection with HIV, it may be many years before someone discovers they are HIV positive or look ill. There is no cure or vaccine and virtually everyone with AIDS dies. HIV is nearly everywhere in the world now, though parts of Africa, India and Southeast Asia have many more infected people than elsewhere. The fear and stigma associated with AIDS have led many Christians to ignore Jesus' teaching and example about compassion, self-interest and judgement. (NB If you think AIDS is God's judgement on homosexuals, then explain why there are more infected children in the world than all the infected gay men, whilst lesbians and nuns have been almost totally spared?)

You **can catch HIV through**:

– Unsafe sexual practices.
– Exchange of infected body fluids through cuts or sores in the skin, mouth (e.g. shared toothbrush) or genitals.
– Sharing unsterilised needles, syringes and sharp instruments used on others (drug users, tattooing, ear piercing, reused medical equipment).
– Transfusion of infected blood or blood products.
– Transplantation of infected body parts.
– Mother to baby before and during birth and breast feeding.

You **can't catch HIV through**:

– Normal social contacts (hugging, holding hands, kissing—usually not even 'French kissing', sharing cutlery).
– The environment (air conditioning/ventilation, coughs, sneezes, water, pools, toilet seats, bed linen, clothes, food, sweat).
– Insect or animal bites.

Avoid it by:

– Celibacy or remaining faithful to a non-infected spouse.
– Using 'universal precautions' (rubber gloves etc.) when dealing with any body fluids including *all* untested people.
– Not receiving untested blood or body products.

– Using 'once-only' medical equipment, perhaps taken with you (see Interhealth for portable AIDS kits and advice).

Reduce your risk by:

– Practising safer sex with any other sexual partner (use condoms, non-penetrating acts, etc.)
– Disinfecting shared needles and syringes, etc.
– Joining a 'walking blood bank' of colleagues for emergency transfusion in high-risk areas with inadequate HIV blood testing facilities (NB you can't guarantee their status).
– Having appropriate vaccinations and anti-malarials, to reduce your need for possibly unsafe hospital equipment overseas.
– Not getting drunk or drug taking (unsafe sex more likely).
– Avoiding road accidents (most likely cause of blood transfusion overseas) by using safe vehicles and drivers; not driving at night or without local driving experience.

Read The Truth About AIDS[1] for more extensive information.

MEMOS

What is the local situation?

Note your blood group

Note the walking blood bank contact procedure (if a member):

1 *Patrick Dixon*, The Truth About AIDS, Third edition 1994, Kingsway Publications, Eastbourne.

CLIMATE

Heat in the tropics needs weeks for full acclimatization.

- **Heat Stroke (overheating) is an Emergency**. Cool down by exposing skin and water evaporation and get medical help.
- **Heat Exhaustion (dehydration)** needs fluids and rest. (In high heat, you may normally need 4–8 litres per day).

Sunshine damages you more near the equator and at altitude, more so if also reflecting off water, sand or snow.

- **Sun burn** may need burns treatment. Prevent by limiting exposure, covering up and using high strength sun bloc.
- **Skin cancer and premature skin ageing** are more likely to follow many years after sun bathing or sun burn.

Altitude (above 9,500 feet) needs gradual acclimatization.

- **Altitude Sickness is an Emergency**. Go back down urgently.
- **Hypothermia (cold) is an Emergency**. Immediately seek shelter and rewarm. Use proper preparation and equipment.

SKIN

With humidity, sweat, heat, sun burn, poorer hygiene, scratching, insect bites, exotic skin bugs, etc., skin infections are much more likely.

- Wash often (including clothes) using clean water and soap.
- Disinfect cuts and abrasions much more carefully than normal and keep off flies but expose them to fresh air.
- Don't burst blisters.
- Take some talcum powder. Avoid cosmetics and deodorants.
- Consider taking a soothing cream like Calamine lotion, an anti-histamine cream for irritating insect bites and some athlete's foot treatment for fungal rashes.

IMMUNISATIONS

You may encounter a wide range of new viruses and bacteria. Talk to a Travel clinic about what is recommended for your destination. You will have to pay for some of them. Some countries require certain immunisation certificates (see **Vital legal issues**). Some immunisations require a course of injections over a number of months. Seek advice at least three months before departure, if possible. Sometimes, you can take booster doses overseas with you (stored in a fridge) to be given by a health professional in due course.

Some virus immunisations: Polio, Hepatitis A, Hepatitis B, Rabies,[a] Yellow Fever, Japanese Encephalitis, Rubella.

Some bacteria immunisations: Tetanus, Diphtheria,[b] BCG (for Tuberculosis), Typhoid, Meningitis, Cholera.[c]

[a]Booster doses required if bitten by a suspect animal

[b]Now becoming a real problem in the former Soviet Union

[c](The older cholera vaccine is not very effective and may be refused by your GP, but countries requiring a certificate may inject you on arrival with unsterile equipment.)

Bear in mind that many important diseases (including Sexually Transmitted ones) have no immunisations.

PARASITES

Microscopic ones include Malaria, Leishmaniasis, Trypanosomiasis (all by insect bites) and Amoebae in water.
Insects (Jiggers) or maggots (Tumbu fly) in your skin.
Food-borne Worms include Tapeworms and Roundworms.
Water-borne Worms include Hookworm and Bilharzia.
External include Leeches and Vampire Bats!

MEMOS

Write a checklist of equipment to take out, if potentially entering extreme environments. Use pages 96–97 below.

Note required immunisations and injection schedules:

DANGEROUS ANIMALS

Snakes and Arthropods—Scorpions, Spiders, Centipedes

If you have to kill a snake, crush its head with a long stout stick (preferably pin it behind the head with a forked stick first). If you are bitten, remember that many snakes are not poisonous and many of the rest won't give you much venom. Few arthropods are dangerously poisonous. It is unlikely you will die, though anxiety symptoms may add to those of the poison. There are two main poisons, one causing bleeding, the other muscle and nerve problems. There may also be tissue damage around the bite. All snake bites with two larger front punctures are by poison injectors. The rest (if poisonous) rely on chewing poison saliva into the bite. Arthropods all inject.

Prevention: Don't put feet into shoes or beds and hands into piles of wood, debris or holes, without checking for inhabitants! Don't enter low vegetation at night, without stout shoes. Beat with a stick to scare snakes ahead.

Treatment: Quickly wipe off surface venom with a clean cloth. Disinfect the wound and dress it. Wrap the entire limb with a firm bandage (don't stop the pulses) and immobilise it to prevent poison being worked deeper into tissues. **NEVER CUT OR SUCK THE WOUND**—infection and tissue damage is all you'll achieve. **NEVER USE A TOURNIQUET**—it may cause gangrene and suddenly releasing it will flood the blood with toxic body chemicals, which might stop the heart. Carry to hospital for observation. (Don't panic.) Anti-venom requires correct identification (kill the snake) and may be dangerous. Only give where adrenaline is also available.

Sea Creatures

When swimming, avoid the dark and keep feet off the bottom or wear rubber soled footwear. Over coral or rocks, use a face mask to enjoy (and avoid) creatures better. **Jellyfish** can cause severe stings, **Conch Shells** can shoot a poison dart. Don't touch spiny **Sea Urchins** or fish—particularly on the bottom (**Stingrays** and **Stonefish**) or with fan-like fins and brown and white stripes (**Lionfish**). Avoid holes (**Moray Eels**), **Sea Snakes** and **Fire Corals** (don't touch any coral if unsure). Seek local information about **Sharks**, which can attack in shallow water, possibly preferring splashers, surfers and menstruating women. Get out if you cut yourself.

DISABILITY AND HEALTH

There are four aspects to weigh up: *Functional level* (degree of self-care, special needs, healthcare needs, mobility and communication skills); *destination* (travel, contingencies, toilets, accommodation and climate); *Organisers* (bias, programme objectives, appropriate planning, venue Hosts); *your resilience* (sometimes increased prejudice, or reduced expectations overseas). Few Organisers run trips to cater for those who are not fully healthy, self-caring, self-mobile and communicative. This is partly because of needing the ability to travel alone in emergency, partly because of ultra-basic living conditions in many venues and partly because there is little pressure to provide opportunities. For helpful travel advice, contact the Disabled Living Foundation (0171–289 6111). **NB Travelling against medical advice will void your medical insurance**.

MEMOS

Note Disability or Health issues to be followed up or maintained:

WOMEN'S NEEDS

Hygiene and Periods

With increased dust, humidity, heat and insufficient clean water and toilets, you may find hygiene more important and less easy. Combined with dehydration, you may find yourself more prone to Cystitis and Candida infections. At the very least, ensure you drink enough to pass clear urine as often as at home, if not more often. Many places do not have tampons or sanitary towels to buy, so take an ample supply or ask advice from a woman who has been where you are going.

Contraception

Again, take adequate supplies for the full time. Avoid the inconvenience of a bleed by not taking the break between packs of Combined pills. (Talk to your GP if you want to do this more than once.) If you rely on condoms, take an adequate supply as local ones may be unsafe or non-existent.

Pregnancy

Airlines have week limits up to which they will carry you. Contact them for advice. The rigours of long distance travel may cause problems with ankle swelling, blood clots, nausea, dehydration and seating/sleeping positions. Some vaccines and anti-malarials may have to be avoided. New or underlying medical conditions may be difficult to treat and important ante-natal checks may be missed. Complications including premature labour could be harder to deal with. Travel insurance usually rules out paying for pregnancy related problems. Talk to your GP. Finally, British citizenship of babies born overseas may be adversely affected.

MEMOS

Is it worth taking any antibiotics or creams for infections?

What First Aid equipment will be taken? (Talk to the Organisers or to Interhealth if nothing is organised.)

FIRST AID

I recommend a First Aid course for remote areas and building work, or a Life Saving course for supervising children near water. This is not a training manual.

But remember—**DR ABC:**

D. DANGER – Check your safety in approaching a casualty.
  – Move them only if still in further danger.
R. ROUSE – See if they're rousable (if so, go to E,F,G,H).
A. AIRWAY – Remove throat blockages.
B. BREATHING – Check mouth with your ear and watch chest.
  – **IF NOT, USE MOUTH TO MOUTH RESUSCITATION:**
  1. Pull jaw forward to pull tongue off throat.
  2. Inflate their lungs with 2 quick breaths.
  3. Check **C – CIRCULATION**; if okay, continue:
  4. Inflate over 2 seconds, release for 3.
  5. Repeat this cycle till breathing starts.
C. CIRCULATION – Check one side only for neck pulse.
  – **IF NOT USE CARDIO-PULMONARY RESUSCITATION (CPR):**
  If working alone:
  1. Give 15 chest compressions (80 a minute).
  2. Give 2 breathing cycles (see B4. above).
  3. Continue the 15:2 cycle till hopeless.
  In pairs: Use a 5:1 cycle. Swap if tired.
D. DROWNING – Few inhale water! Good resuscitation chances.
E. BLEEDING – Firmly press wound; raise legs; **NO TOURNIQUETS.**
F. FRACTURES/DISLOCATIONS – Splint joints above and below.
G. NECK/BACK BRACING for all Trauma or Fall casualties and **RECOVERY POSITION** for unconscious, non-Trauma ones.
H. HOSPITAL for anyone from **A–G** or temporarily unconscious.

Situations likely to severely stress anyone include: Witness to a traumatic death; seeing mutilated bodies; seeing a dead child; expecting sudden death; violence against yourself; witnessing violence against others; witnessing extreme pain; being under fire; incarceration; interrogation; any extreme fear. You may find yourself involved in a sudden (Acute) or ongoing (Chronic) stressful situation. You might go on to develop symptoms of Post Trauma Stress Syndrome.

ACUTE MAJOR STRESS

Coping –   *For a few hours only*: Keep active; suppress emotion; avoid unnecessary sights; work on 'autopilot'; limit necessary exposure; allow 'black humour' with colleagues; deny reality.
For drawn-out situations: Stop above methods; talk with colleagues and supervisors about what you've seen and done; take breaks together; don't neglect yourselves.

Problems –   Someone in 'Shock' may be motionless, apathetic, helpless and behaving strangely.

Treatment – For someone in 'Shock': Keep physical contact; prevent isolation; remove responsibilities; talk to them; seek professional care.

CHRONIC MAJOR STRESS

Coping –   Don't become isolated; learn some of the local language; pamper yourself a little; maintain a pleasant living environment; don't neglect your health and habits; eat well; avoid alcohol; take regular short breaks; maintain spiritual life; 'Defuse' with colleagues—talk about difficult situations and feelings; consider having a 'Buddy'—monitor each other's coping (or not); seek help early for yourself and colleagues.

Problems –   Someone approaching 'Burnout' may appear: superhuman; snowed-under; unwilling to take breaks; exhausted; depressed; anxious; restless; deluded; paranoid; manic; suicidal.

Treatment – Depending on the degree of problem, they may need a short holiday, permanent withdrawal, counselling or psychiatric assessment.

POST-TRAUMA STRESS SYNDROME[1]

This is not predictable, but is more likely with more severe incidents (maybe a quarter of survivors in the worst scenarios).

Prevention – No personal history of major psychosis or neurosis helps; 'Defusing' straight after the incident; a 'Buddy' system for longer term situations; 'Critical Incident Debriefing' more than 24 hours after the situation ends (Interhealth can find trained CID debriefers.)

Symptoms – For one to two months after the end or the peak of an incident, *anyone normal might face*: Depression; flashbacks; avoidance behaviours; disturbed sleep; nightmares; 'jumpiness'; 'survivor guilt'; anger, despair, sorrow, etc.

Problems – Persisting or worsening symptoms; deteriorating significant relationships; disrupted lifestyle.

Treatment – Counselling or psychiatric care.

MEMOS

If under chronic stress, outline and keep reviewing your coping strategies:

In the memo pages at the end of this book, record details of the worst aspect of any major incident, to prompt recall and hopefully prevent repressed memories leading to depression and post-traumatic stress disorder:

1 *Frank Parkinson*, Post Trauma Stress, 1993, Sheldon Press.

POSITIVE EFFECTS
- The spiritual challenge may deepen your relationship with God and with other Christians.
- You may discover for the first time, how insular, parochial and small-minded you and your culture are.
- The contrast in living conditions may force you to change your own lifestyle and perhaps, to begin to challenge the economic and political systems involved.
- You may develop a yearning to return overseas; perhaps as a Missionary, development worker, educationalist or on further Short Term programmes—even as a Leader.
- You might want to emphasise the global aspect of the World Church; perhaps as a volunteer representative or by looking for work in UK offices of overseas concerns.

Our research at Tear Fund[1] suggests that over two thirds of Participants return very challenged and excited.

ANTICLIMAX
Within a short time, many feel this. It is quite natural.

- The sudden removal of stress may leave you with withdrawal symptoms—perhaps you feel bored without it.
- You may have become a bit dependent on each other. Suddenly you have to live with yourself as your main company. Who needs you now?
- You might be really missing close friends.
- You might be thrown back into difficult circumstances or responsibilities.
- Maybe you're relieved (or guilty) to be back; letting go your coping mechanisms may release a flood of emotion.

We found that two fifths became a little sad and cynical.

REVERSE CULTURE SHOCK
Quite a few people face emotional turmoil on return.[2]

- You might feel 'homesick' for the place and people.
- You might be daunted by the fast Western approach to life.
- You may feel angry at Western culture: greed, consumerism, cynicism, lack of family and community values.
- You could feel bewildered at the supermarket choice or change since last here, or alienated from society.
- You often find few people genuinely interested in your time overseas. This can lead to isolation or resentment.

Our research suggests that a fifth of Short-Termers are depressed and tearful within a few weeks after return.

SUPPORT

- The best tonic is to renew relationships and share common experiences, particularly since returning, with those who went with you. If a reunion is not organised for you, then make sure you arrange one yourself; at least overnight.
- Also, find someone locally who can appreciate your experiences, before you become cynical—perhaps an ex-Missionary. If your church was supportive before you went, share with them in an appropriate context. (Don't distance people with a boring slide presentation.)
- If you do feel depressed or can't cope, seek professional help early, perhaps through a counsellor or your GP.

MEMOS

Note your responses to the following questions on returning and review them again three months later, or just prior to a reunion (also refer back to your personal Spiritual Objectives):

List positive outcomes:

List negative outcomes:

1 *'Ditch' Townsend*, Unpublished, Verbal Presentation to the 2nd Conference of Short Term Programme Organisers, 1994, Tear Fund (UK).
2 *Peter Jordan*, Re-Entry—Making the Transition from Missions to Life at Home, 1992, YWAM, Vancouver.

As a Short Term trip Organiser, I was constantly amazed by the way people's lives changed during a summer overseas. Let seeing the world change your life. Don't let it submerge as a one off opportunity, to chalk down against experience (or worse—your token gesture to God's call to Mission).

MOVING ON
- Build on new insights into God's character and developments in your relationship with him. Pray for those involved in Mission and the situation you've left behind.
- A number of people return on future Short Term programmes. Try to keep learning each time. Have some purpose beyond just more 'good times'; make your trips part of someone else's learning experience.
- Develop the skills and experience needed to be a Deputy or full Team Leader; a vital resource for new Participants.
- Offer voluntary representation to the Organisation you have travelled with, perhaps locally or more widely, or to other Organisations you're in sympathy with.
- Begin to fund (or fundraise for) these Organisations.
- Consider maintaining or developing long term relationships with someone overseas. Consider this also, on behalf of a group you are in (church, school, college, etc.)
- Consolidate your training and experience, so as to offer yourself for full time overseas service. (Talk to the Christian Service Centre for advice.) Almost any vocation or profession can provide a useful background, with additional training—at home and overseas.
- Investigate Bible college or a Mission training college as a serious option.
- Consider working in the UK office of an overseas focused Organisation, or as a full time communicator.
- Write about your experiences in a readable, interesting way—for a local paper, church magazine, or something with a wider readership.
- Educate yourself further about world issues, through newspapers, magazines, documentaries, part time courses.
- Involve yourself in world issues, through writing to the media or politicians about topical subjects you care about and can give a personal angle on.
- Give thought to personal involvement in the media or politics. Consider joining pressure groups such as Amnesty International or the World Development Movement.

MEMOS

Monitor your progress or demise, in making long term use of your overseas experiences:

Against each item, place an X in the first column if you need to deal with the issue. Place an X in the second column when it is achieved. (I have placed an X next to those items I think are essential regardless of destination.)

APPLICATION

[X] [   ] I know what I'm getting myself into.
[X] [   ] I have balanced my need for faith with preparation.
[X] [   ] I know reasonable theological justifications.
[X] [   ] I have good reasons for wanting to apply.
[X] [   ] I know my specific Aims and Objectives.
[X] [   ] I know what trip to look for and where to find it.
[X] [   ] I can't rule myself out before applying.
[   ] [   ] Deposits, application and reference forms sent.
[   ] [   ] Selection arranged and prepared for.
[   ] [   ] Employers informed or unpaid leave requested.
[   ] [   ] Choice between offers made and Organisers informed.

SUPPORT

[X] [   ] Family and friends adequately talked with.
[X] [   ] Christian fellowship willing to support.
[X] [   ] Organisers adequately prepared and responsible.
[X] [   ] Expenditure fully budgeted.
[X] [   ] Funding sorted out.

LEGAL ISSUES

[X] [ ] Passport	[X] [ ] Medical Insurance
[ ] [ ] Travel Insurance	[ ] [ ] Life insurance
[ ] [ ] Visa	[ ] [ ] Medical certificates
[ ] [ ] E111	[ ] [ ] Work permit
[ ] [ ] Import/export	[ ] [ ] National Insurance
[ ] [ ] Tax	[ ] [ ] Power of Attorney
[ ] [ ] Will	[ ] [ ] Overseas Voter register
[ ] [ ] Child Benefit	[ ] [ ] Unemployment benefit
[ ] [ ] Housing Benefit	[ ] [ ] Social Security
[ ] [ ] Council Tax	[ ] [ ] Gas
[ ] [ ] Electricity	[ ] [ ] Telephone
[ ] [ ] Credit cards	[ ] [ ] Rent
[ ] [ ] Mortgage	[ ] [ ] Court, Probation, Fines

COMMUNICATIONS

[X] [ ] System to home worked out	[ ] [ ] Back up to home
[X] [ ] System to you worked out	[ ] [ ] Back up to you
[ ] [ ] Radio and frequencies	[ ] [ ] Prayer letters

INTERNAL PREPARATION

[X] [   ] Not too stressed to go   [?] [   ] Feel ready to go
[X] [   ] Self aware   [?] [   ] Hobby
[X] [   ] Can handle conflict   [   ] [   ] Role preferences
[X] [   ] Culturally prepared   [X] [   ] Team relationship ex-
[X] [   ] Spiritually prepared   pectations understood

GENERAL PREPARATION

(*At least soon after arrival)

[X] [   ] *Currency regulations   [X] [   ] *The Task
[X] [   ] *Inflation & Exchange rates   [X] [   ] Spending money
[X] [   ] Know your Organisation   [X] [   ] The Project
[X] [   ] Team has >1 cash source   [X] [   ] The Country
[X] [   ] Travel plans   [   ] [   ] Local bureaucracy
[   ] [   ] Driving needs   [   ] [   ] Travel guide book
[X] [   ] National Religions   [X] [   ] *National church

SECURITY

[   ] [   ] Security devices   [   ] [   ] EVACUATION PLAN

MEMOS

MEDICAL

[X] [   ] Additional information   [   ] [   ] Anti-malarials
[X] [   ] Insurance contact number   [X] [   ] Blood Group
[   ] [   ] Walking Blood Bank   [   ] [   ] AIDS Kit
[?] [   ] Medical check up   [   ] [   ] Skin medications
[   ] [   ] Immunisations   [   ] [   ] Special equipment
[   ] [   ] Other medications   [   ] [   ] Tampons/Pads
[   ] [   ] Contraceptives & condoms   [   ] [   ] First Aid course
[X] [   ] First Aid kit if not supplied
            by Organisers

FOLLOW UP

[X] [   ] Reunion & Friendships   [   ] [   ] Overseas contacts
[   ] [   ] Opportunities to share   [X] [   ] Support
[   ] [   ] Voluntary representative   [X] [   ] Changed life

KIT LIST

Devise your own, to include clothing and equipment suitable for culture (work, leisure and church), climate (including relevant extreme climates), hygiene, hobbies and local technological development. Also, necessary insect protection and water purification. Consider luggage and its weight:

[ ]   [ ]

[ ]   [ ]

[ ]   [ ]

[ ]   [ ]

[ ]   [ ]

[ ]   [ ]

[ ]   [ ]

[ ]   [ ]

[ ]   [ ]

[ ]   [ ]

[ ]   [ ]

[ ]   [ ]

[ ]   [ ]

[ ]   [ ]

[ ]   [ ]

[ ]   [ ]

[ ]   [ ]

[ ]   [ ]

[ ]   [ ]

[ ]   [ ]

[ ]   [ ]

[ ]   [ ]

[ ]   [ ]

[ ]   [ ]

[ ]   [ ]

[ ]   [ ]
[ ]   [ ]
[ ]   [ ]
[ ]   [ ]
[ ]   [ ]
[ ]   [ ]
[ ]   [ ]
[ ]   [ ]
[ ]   [ ]
[ ]   [ ]
[ ]   [ ]
[ ]   [ ]
[ ]   [ ]
[ ]   [ ]
[ ]   [ ]
[ ]   [ ]
[ ]   [ ]
[ ]   [ ]
[ ]   [ ]
[ ]   [ ]
[ ]   [ ]
[ ]   [ ]
[ ]   [ ]
[ ]   [ ]
[ ]   [ ]
[ ]   [ ]
[ ]   [ ]
[ ]   [ ]
[ ]   [ ]
[ ]   [ ]
[ ]   [ ]
[ ]   [ ]
[ ]   [ ]

SOURCES OF LEADERS

Leaders may become associated with a Team through a number of diverse routes, with associated drawbacks, including:

- *Being part of the original organisational set-up.* (Are you really the most appropriate? Who could prevent you going? A discerning external appraisal may be a wise move.)
- *Being drawn in (willingly or not) from another part of the Organisation,* under your job description. (Do you have the motivation to work effectively in this role?)
- *Being seconded for the job, from a Partner Organisation*—at home or overseas. (Is this a 'politically correct' manoeuvre, or are you really the right person?)
- *Having grown through 'the ranks' on past Teams,* sometimes with other Organisations. (Do you really have enough experience or maturity? Persuading non-experts of your abilities may be easier than you think. Or maybe desperate Organisers will take anyone who vaguely fits the bill?)
- *Being 'creamed off' from the crop of ordinary Applicants.* (Again, are you really suitable or is it a cheaper, easier way of finding Leaders? Will you accept just because you're so amazed to have been asked?)
- *Being invited 'cold' to lead,* on the grounds of perceived experience or accomplishments. (Is it your ability or your name, which is wanted? Have you weighed up the practical work, preparation and responsibility it may involve?)

Organisational match

The Organisation may not select you with adequate thoroughness: Are you up to the job? Do you know what it is? Do you share their goals and visions? Do you agree with their policies, procedures and practice? Can you represent their interests sufficiently, overseas? (There, you may be seen to personify the Organisation; will you instead caricature it?) Will you be 'cut loose' or on a 'tight leash'? Are all the emergency and contingency systems adequate for your level of experience or the Team's needs? Does going fit in with your plans, or will you have to drop something important to say yes? Will you be expected to contribute significantly to the pre-departure organisation? (Will it all be dumped on you?) Do you meet the criteria expected of ordinary Applicants? These should all be issues Organisers consider before they select you.

Training

The Organisers should brief you on the following, with specific reference to your venue and their expectations:

Their Aims and Objectives	Their Organisation
Travel, Delays and Driving	Finance and Security
Partners/Hosts/Local church	Project/Work
Your Authority and Role	Team Discipline
The Team Members	Local Bureaucracy
Local Culture, Climate etc.	Local Board and Lodging
Holidays; Independent travelling	Insurance
Inter-personal Relationships	Spiritual issues
Communication systems	Medical issues
Emergencies	Your Support

MEMOS

How are you being drawn into leadership?

What is your motivation?

List your skills and weaknesses:

Outline your Training needs:

What do you know about the Organisation you will represent?

BORN LEADER?

The success of a Team depends on several interwoven factors including: *goals, individuals, leadership, 'team dynamic', preparation* and *operational circumstances*. Any of these can unbalance the Team (or be made the 'scapegoat' for failure). Defining some of these factors reduces options for others; the Leader's role will vary and his/her preferred style may not fit requirements. **NB: Don't forget delegation**.

PREFERRED STYLES

Research indicates four broad styles, which Leaders may use to varying degrees (from circumstance to circumstance or between different Leaders in the same context):

1. *Commander.* You issue orders to be followed, with little questioning. You may be the expert, the work simple, or discipline, morale and time are paramount. Everything is task-centred. If the job is successful, Team satisfaction may balance out resentment, unless they feel demeaned or that the task didn't require such subservience.
2. *Hidden Persuader.* You use a whole armoury of mechanisms to get people to do what you want, including empathy, cajoling, rewarding, manipulating, arguing. If all else fails, you threaten. When the task is achieved, this can have less 'fall-out' from the Team, but it takes time.
3. *Prime Minister.* After allowing Team members' ideas full ventilation and discussion, you use them to modify your own ones, before announcing the way forward. Some may feel let down if their views aren't incorporated, but most will feel more satisfied with such participation. However, it takes even more time and the result may be a tangle of misguided compromises.
4. *Shop Steward.* You see your job as simply oiling decision making. Whether or not you agree, you will abide by the majority wish, though the process may be interminable. Whilst this is more democratic, ignoring isolated but correct opinion in favour of the majority can lead to failure. This may lead to resentment, not least if you knew it would go wrong, but overruled your own authority.

PROBABLE ROLES

Authority and Responsibility. You will probably take responsibility for decisions and discipline, particularly where the Organisers cannot be easily contacted.

Courier and Accountant. If travel is chaotic or complicated, a co-ordinator is vital. Also, for audit purposes. you may be personally responsible for communal budgeting.

Work Supervisor. You will need to co-ordinate communal chores, cooking, shopping, etc. and liaise between work supervisors and the Team (or act as supervisor yourself!)

Counsellor. The Team may expect you to cope better, relying on your maturity and experience to offer them caring support and useful advice where necessary.

Pastor. You will need to co-ordinate any Team devotions, monitoring spiritual needs and interfacing with the local church and other Christians, perhaps preaching occasionally.

Chairman. Meetings for updates and discussion are vital.

MEMOS

What kind of leadership role do you prefer and what are its strengths and weaknesses?

Outline your key roles as briefed by the Organisers:

This is a model for leadership within a defined task, developed by the Industrial Society,[1] who have kindly allowed me to reproduce much of it for you. It is less useful for 'off-the-job' leadership and is least suited to someone with a totally democratic style.

THE PROCESS

There are five elements, which follow one another in a cycle before restarting the process as the task proceeds:

1. *Define Objectives*
2. *Plan the Task* (Gather information and decide)
3. *Brief the Team*
4. *Monitor and Support*
5. *Evaluate Performance*

THE ACTIVITIES

The whole process can be defined as a set of key actions, in terms of the Task, the Team and the Individuals:

Actions	Task	Team	Individuals
Define Objectives	Identify tasks and constraints	Hold Team Meeting – share commitment	Clarify objectives and gain acceptance
Plan (Gather info.)	Consider options and check resources	Consult and encourage ideas and develop suggestions and assess skills	
(Decide)	Priorities and time scales and standards	Structure	Allocate jobs – delegate – set targets
Brief	Clarify objectives and describe plan	Explain decisions – listen – answer questions – enthuse – check understanding	
Monitor and support	Assess progress and maintain standards	Co-ordinate and reconcile conflict and recognise effort	Advise/praise and assist/reassure and counsel and discipline
Evaluate	Summarise and review objectives and replan if necessary	Recognise/gain from success and learn from mistakes	Appraise performance
		Guide and train and give praise	

MEMOS

Modify this model, if appropriate, to suit your situation:

1 Action-Centred Leadership Framework, (Available in credit card format: Ref 1 (1989)), Peter Runge House, 3 Carlton House Terrace, London SW1Y 5DG.

WHEN TO HAVE ONE

Not every Team has, or needs a Deputy. At Tear Fund, we felt that Teams with over five Participants, going for more than three weeks to do a practical job in a more remote area, needed a Deputy. It was also considered for any Team travelling where the size of vehicles or light aircraft required the Team to split. (Travel is one of the phases most likely to incur problems needing defined leadership.) It was also important for large or very inexperienced Teams, since more pastoral and administrative leadership is needed.

ADVANTAGES

- A solitary Leader can become quite isolated from the Team, but a Deputy can bridge the gap, sometimes as an advocate for the Team or Leader, to each other.
- A Leader can be cut off following a difficult decision, but a Deputy will back them up.
- Without a Deputy, a Leader may have no personal support or shoulder to cry on when in difficullty.
- The Leader can discuss complex issues confidentially before making a decision, such as on discipline questions.
- Without humiliating the Leader, the Deputy can challenge him/ her regarding errant behaviour or attitudes.
- The Deputy should act as Executive Officer, with permission to challenge and question leadership decisions without fear of reprisal, but ultimately providing full support no matter what the conclusion.
- The Deputy can take over leadership with full authority where necessary; if the Leader is away or ill.
- The Team can be split for travel, independent functions, or alternating jobs/breaks using rotas.
- The Organisers will have selected and prepared the Deputies along with the Leaders and will be able to trust them to take over in emergencies. It saves the Team from trying to elect or follow a self-imposed Leader, at a time when they may also be trying to deal with a crisis.
- The Leader and Deputy may split roles between them, to allow 'specialisation', for instance between the courier and pastoral care functions.

DISADVANTAGES

- Deputies sometimes feel redundant, particularly if there is little they can do or the Leader prefers to work alone.

- Hosts and work supervisors are sometimes unclear about the role of each Leader and it can confuse communication.
- Where there are joint Leaders, the lines of authority can become blurred. Even Team leadership usually needs an appointed Chairman.
- Deputies are sometimes condescended to by Leaders, who try to invent jobs for them to do.
- Some Deputies feel overburdened by having all administrative tasks delegated to them, leaving decisions and 'juicy' jobs for the Leader.
- The Deputy may occasionally assume responsibility from under the Leader's nose, perhaps in response to a sort of 'mutiny' by Team members, instead of supporting him/her.

MEMOS

Outline the roles you have negotiated with any other Leaders and update these as required:

GIFTS

Take some simple gifts from home to give away on the Team's behalf (tinned travel sweets, designer tea towels, etc.)

PUBLIC PRESENTATIONS

Prepare or organise the Team to prepare a sermon or two, some simple thematic mimes, some testimonies and choruses (unaccompanied or reliant on Team instruments only). Also, have a prepared speech of greeting and introduction from the Organisers, the UK church and the Team along with another of thanks on the Team and Organiser's behalf. Consider having a 'child-friendly' version too.

Always use simple English. This helps translators. It helps people who only speak simple English. The Good News Bible uses the right words. Don't put four ideas in a sentence. Compare this paragraph with the one before. This one is simpler. It also repeats words.

TRAVEL

See the later **Emergencies** page 3.2.5). Also, see the sections for PARTICIPANTS: 2.2.3, 2.4.4, 2.4.5, 2.4.9, 2.5.0. Arranging travel is covered later in the section for ORGANISERS. In addition:

- If the Organisers haven't reserved specific seats after confirming the booking, you may be able to do so by phone.
- Check in at least two hours before flights. (**NB: Local traffic!**).
- Reconfirm all return flights for the Team, 72 hours before expected return (and never less than 48 hours before).
- Double check that the return flight is not cancelled or delayed, before leaving for the airport.
- Double check before leaving, that everyone has passports, all necessary documents, certificates, bags and tickets.
- If specific seats aren't already reserved, ensure the Team checks in together and that there are enough seats left, before the first lot of luggage goes through. The earlier you check in, the more likely the group can sit together.
- Checking in three–four hours before an international flight back, will usually allow you to beat the crush and avoid being bumped off an overbooked flight.
- The departure lounge, after check-in, is usually the most comfortable (airconditioned) place to wait at an airport.
- Report missing baggage immediately to the airline (get written acknowledgement), for insurance claims.
- Know the *street address* and phone number of your destination or the person meeting you at the airport.

REST

You and the Team will not function for long on 'nervous energy'. Don't encourage persistent early mornings or late nights. Don't push daily work beyond reasonable limits. Take two hour lunch breaks in the heat. Prevent those with diarrhoea or other minor illnesses from working. Go out together as a Team, perhaps taking a weekend or week off, particularly if the Team has become demoralised or 'tetchy'.

MEMOS

Plan a few gifts to take:

Outline key points for a speech of *Greeting* or *Introduction*:

Outline a few key points for a speech of *Thanks*:

For general advice, read the sections for PARTICIPANTS: 2.2.2, 2.4.1.

TEAM FUNDS

You will probably carry a float of money from the Organisers on behalf of the Team, for various direct costs. You may also carry a contingency fund, for immediate medical and urgent travel expenses. If any Team cash is insured, it may only be so in the hands of a Leader. Remember to sign all travellers cheques once, before departure (usually on collection). Don't allow another Team member to sign some. Look after any credit cards with care.

AUDIT

Any charity will have its accounts subjected to an annual audit. You will be accountable for the portion of funds put in your care. Don't mix personal and Team accounts, nor wait till you get home to try and sort it out.

– Count all currency given to you in front of the Organisation representative, before taking custody of it.
– Obtain receipts for every currency exchange.
– Also for every expenditure (except small items like stationary, drinks, snacks, short taxi journeys).
– Make Team members sign for all personal currency advances.
– Maintain a daily cash flow booklet.

CASH FLOW

Use a notebook with something like the following model:

Section 1—Foreign Currency (UK£, US$, etc.)
CASH. (Repeat for TRAVELLERS CHEQUES, TRANSFERS, etc.)

Date	Amount	Remainder	Exchange Rate	Notes
4.7.95	+US$500	US$500		Received
5.7.95	−US$150	US$350	US$1=ZIM$5.23	Exchanged
6.8.95	−US$50	US$300	Loaned to J. Smith:	Signed . . .
7.9.95	+US$45.74	US$345.74	US$1=ZIM$5.41	Re-exchanged
				(−1% Charge)
8.9.95	−US$75	US$270.74		Airport Tax
				in US$

Section 2—Local Currency (e.g. ZIM$)

Date	In/Out	Total	Notes
5.7.95	+776.65	776.65	From US$ Cash (−1% Charge)
5.7.95	−100	676.65	Two taxis to town T

(T=Travel, A=Accommodation, F=Food & Drinks, W=Work, O=Other)

At the end, rewrite cash flow in columns for Exchanges, Travel, Accomodation etc., on a neat sheet. NB: Account for Foreign Currency spent without exchange (e.g. US$ Airport Tax) as a local Currency in its own right with a 1:1 rate of exchange.

EXPENDITURE ACCOUNT

Your final front sheet, with attached Cash Flow compilation, receipts, remaining cash, travellers cheques and personal cheques might look like:

Currency:	Received	Exchanged	Reexchanged	Spent	Other	Returned
US$ Cash	+500.00	−150.00	+45.74	−75.00	−50.00	+270.74
ZIM$ Cash	0.00	+776.65	−250.00	−518.10	0.00	+8.55

MEMOS

Consider compiling a copy of your final accounts below, or in the memo pages at the end of this book for reference when tying up finances with the Organisers:

Unless you are simply courier for a package holiday in disguise, there will potentially be circumstances where an individual's behaviour reflects negatively on the Team, Organisation or Hosts.

WARNINGS

The Organisation should have briefed you and Participants on the range of possible misdemeanours and any sanctions which could be applied. These will vary between Organisations. Where Organisers have undertaken to provide services, it is clearly unreasonable to withdraw them without adequate warning and support. Attention should have been drawn to the issue before ever money was handed over. Whilst they are not merely clients, Participants are not employees either and can't simply be dismissed, nor could they if they were. It is hoped that you can exercise the option of warning miscreants, without sudden, summary judgement. They will also need fair punishment. You would be unwise to act alone.

ADVICE

Talk to your Deputy and seek the confidential advice of wise local Christian Leaders, particularly if you are working in partnership with a local Host Organisation. Discuss the situation with the Organisers back home if possible; and without fail if you wish to ask someone to go home, despite extravagant phone/fax charges.

ASSISTANCE

Don't act unreasonably. At the very least, if you are going to request that someone leave the Team, they should have their own passport and ticket. They will require funds to make the journey back to the airport, pay for altered flight arrangements, plus any food and accommodation along the way. They should be assisted as necessary, with translation, administrative help and any other facilities they may have relied on you and the Team for. Having offered all this, if the Participant chooses to shun assistance, then make a written record of what was offered, signed if possible by them or an available witness.

POSSIBLE ISSUES

The following is by no means comprehensive, nor will all of them require removal of those involved:

- Cultural insensitivity
- Flaunting agreed rules
- Negative spiritual issues
- Not 'pulling their weight'

- Disruption
- Dangerous behaviour
- Immorality

110

MISINTERPRETING BEHAVIOUR

- You or others may over-emphasise the importance of any given issue, due to stress or misunderstandings.
- Unreasonable behaviour can reflect a mental problem released by stress or illness, particularly psychosis, mania and depression, all needing treatment, not sanctions. In carefully selected Participants, this is possibly the most common reason for repatriation.

MEMOS

Note below any specific disciplinary issues highlighted by the Organisers:

1. RELAX

Anxiety feels very like fear, but does not relate to a specific object. Reactions caused by fear can be useful: so-called 'Fight or Flight'. We switch into overdrive, to deal with a visible threat. Anxiety merely exhausts, without us doing anything very useful. Until you find something tangible to react to, relax. It can be very stressful in itself.

2. ESTABLISH PRIORITIES

– Beware of 'tunnel-vision': of focusing all effort into one aspect of a problem. View the complete picture.
– Keep a balanced perspective on issues and over the whole.
– Define priorities in terms of action, not 'importance'.
   (**Not**: 'x' is crucial and 'y' is reasonably important **but rather**:'x' needs all my attention for two hours with no interruptions and 'y' could be fitted into spare moments tomorrow).
– Adapt this model to fit your needs:

Priority	Resources	Supervision	Review
One	All	Total	Constant
Two	Majority	3hrs in 4	Hourly
Three	Half	1hr in 4	2x daily
Four	A quarter	1hr a day	2 days
Five	Essential only	2hrs a week	Weekly
Six	Minimal	Occasional	Fortnightly

(NB Remember Deadlines and Team members' needs)

3. SET OPERATIONAL GOALS

There are a number of ways to approach a crisis and it is worth defining yours. Likely ones include:

Maintenance: preserving things as they are.

Adaptation: managing change to fit new circumstances.

Retrieval: taking time to restore normality if possible; concentrating on the worst issues first and others later.

Salvage: preserving only the most important things; abandoning the worst, time consuming problems.

4. STEPS TO TAKE

The ensuing model may not suit every circumstance, but is akin to other 'Problem-Solving' approaches:

1. Outline the apparent *effects* of the problem.
2. Gather further, necessary information.
3. Redefine the *effects* of the problem and summarise.
4. Suggest possible *causes* and gather evidence.
5. Rank by decreasing probability/consequence.
6. Tackle possible *causes* in descending order.
7. Devise *solutions* and rank in order of complexity.
8. Implement *solutions*, simplest ones first.
9. Define *outcomes*, in terms of timing and goals.
10. Monitor *outcomes* at pre-arranged times.
11. *Modify* the process, but only at reviews or if urgent.

MEMOS

(Copy this page onto note paper and start a 'Crisis File')

A) Don't panic!

B) Allocate priorities to Issues and update as necessary:

Priority	Date	Issue	Notes

C) Outline your Operational Goals:

D) Dealing with the Crisis:
(1–3) How has the problem manifested itself?

(4–6) Rank causes in order of probability/consequence:

(7–8) Rank solutions in order of complexity:

(9–10) Define *Outcomes*, including major review times:

Goal	Timing

[Relevant notes are in the **Discipline** (3.2.3) and **Managing a Crisis** (3.2.4) pages. Also in the **PARTICIPANTS** section under **Communication Systems** (2.2.5), **Driving** (2.4.5), **Personal Security** (2.4.9), **Major Emergencies** (2.4.10) and **Medical Issues**: First Aid and Post Trauma Stress (2.5.5 and 2.5.6).]

COMMUNICATING

Know how to contact the Organisers 24 hours a day. Contact them as soon as possible, if a problem arises.

DELAYS

Airlines must provide free meals and hotel rooms, after a certain period. Stay with other passenges, near the airline desk for updates. They should offer free facilities to contact anyone meeting you. All this also applies to overbooked flights, where you are 'bumped' off. EC airlines within the EC are obliged to provide a full refund and free flight if overbooked. Tell the Organisers.

REARRANGING TRAVEL

Depending on your ticket, you may possibly change flights with varying penalties. The cheapest APEX ones allow no alterations. Some require a supplement to be paid. If you miss a flight, talk to the airline. If they won't help, get appropriate documents, if this is covered by insurance and re-book. Try to phone and cancel a flight; 'no-shows' are usually penalised. Standby may be possible but is worrying and not always successful. Sometimes, airlines will endorse your ticket, to fly on another airline (they transfer payment). This is most likely if they have an agreement with other airlines or if a delay or cancellation is their fault.

MEDICAL EMERGENCIES

1. First, seek urgent, adequate medical care.
2. Second, contact the insurers, to ensure they will pay.
3. Third, contact the Organisers and UK medical advisers to provide additional medical history and support.

The insurers may decide to send an Air Ambulance or to pay for urgent return (perhaps with three or four seats) for a 'walking wounded'. If (except to save life) you don't talk to them until after expensive major surgery and intensive care are under way, they may later refuse to pay. Possibly the cost of chartering a private plane, Doctor and Nurse may be cheaper than surgery and two days' intensive care overseas!

DEATH

You will probably feel overwhelmed and under-prepared. Contact the Insurers and the local British representative for advice. It may be best to involve a local undertaker, who will know what to do while arrangements for cremation or transport of the body home, are made. The local Police or Coroner's office may need to be informed, particularly if the death was due to accident, violence or unexplained. If concerned about the cause of death, consider having the body flown home for post-mortem. There may be an inquest in the UK. The press may be interested; protect the family and use only a single press contact, preferably a senior Organiser.

MEMOS

Well before leaving, note issues you need to prepare for and find out a bit more about what to do in each situation:

Keep a 'Crisis File' of carefully compiled, dated entries of key circumstances, decisions and reasons for them, signing each one as if a legal record, throughout a major crisis. Keep any documents relating to the problem.

(You may find aspects of the notes for **PARTICIPANTS** 2.6.1 **On Return** and 2.6.2 **The Rest of Your Life** useful.)

FAILURE

You will have taken on much more responsibility than most Team members, relying on additional experience, maturity and training. You may also have carried the can for some major situations. It is possible that the Team criticised your leadership, or you felt they did, behind your back. You may know that you made inadequate decisions or over-exerted your authority on occasion. You may have toiled under the knowledge that there were more appropriate, experienced or mature people on the Team, under your leadership. You may have had to deal with unexpected culture shock, home-sickness or situational reactions in yourself. In short, you may feel a bit of a failure, not least if some particular targets or objectives were not met as planned.

SUPPORT

– For all these reasons, a confidential debriefing is crucial, with the Organisers.
– It may be useful to have a private sharing session with other Leaders and Deputies from other projects under the same or similar programme Organisers.
– You may benefit from sharing your experience with someone in your church who is experienced in any form of team leadership, as much to get things off your chest, as to learn from the experience.

ENCOURAGEMENT

Experience with any form of team leadership will remind you that such reactions are frequently encountered, particularly where your own supervisors are unable to be part of your work and its conditions. Criticism from those who haven't tried to operate under similar circumstances, can usually safely be ignored. Furthermore, my experience is that whilst Team members and Leaders both recognise apparent shortcomings in the Team's achievements overseas, in very few cases does anyone blame the Leader, except him/herself. Where the Leader has displayed inadequacies, the Team usually has a good overall experience and the Leader often thinks that he/she did a good job. I suggest that if you hold together an inexperienced Team in a remote area and are given less than a few months, just about any practical achievement is a success! Usually, it is our targets or objectives which are inappropriate.

THE TEAM
- Write to Team members after they have returned, to follow up any problems which may not be picked up by the Organisers and to help them reintegrate, so they don't feel all their friendships, developed over the last few weeks, have just disappeared.
- Attend any organised reunion if possible, or ensure that one is organised, again for the sake of the Team members, if not yourself.

MEMOS

First note any 'gut level' subjective or negative feelings about how you did your job:

Now try to be more objective, taking account of debriefings, facts and positive comments made by anyone concerned:

(**Also for Deputies**). Against each item, place an X in the first column if you need to deal with the issue. Place an X in the second column when it is achieved. (I have placed an X next to those items I think are essential regardless of destination.) *Also* work through the list for Participants.

SELECTION

[X] [   ] I know what is required of me.
[X] [   ] I am capable (through God's grace).
[X] [   ] I am compatible with the Organisation.
[X] [   ] I have received sufficient training.

LEADERSHIP

[X] [   ] I am aware of and can modify my preferred styles.
[X] [   ] I understand my principal roles and how to delegate.
[   ] [   ] Leader and Deputy agree with their functions.

PRACTICAL ISSUES

[   ] [   ] Gifts prepared.
[   ] [   ] Public presentations prepared.
[X] [   ] Travel details understood.
[X] [   ] *Street* address and phone number of overseas contact.
[·X] [   ] Appropriate financial monitoring prepared.
[X] [   ] Sufficient Team funds and contingency, on you.
[X] [   ] Team insurance issues understood.
[X] [   ] Policy agreed with Organiser on Team members wanting to stay on after.

EMERGENCIES

[X] [   ] Disciplinary procedures understood and accepted.
[X] [   ] Prepared to manage a crisis.
[X] [   ] Communication system to Organisers understood.
[X] [   ] Back up communication system.
[X] [   ] Medical emergency procedure agreed with Organisers.

AIMS AND OBJECTIVES
- These should flow from the Organisation's general calling, or 'Mission Statement'. Refer to it or devise one first.
- In them, remember: a) those affected by the Programme in the UK, b) those Overseas and c) the Participants.

VIABILITY
- Before embarking, obtain support from the wider Christian community; sense God's calling; have a servant attitude.
- Then ask yourself if your services are really needed (seek expert, independent advice or consultancy).
- Ensure you have enough resources to start *and* finish.
- Will your Programme grow from current resources or will you need extensive, appropriate training first?
- Can your Programme really involve unskilled volunteers?
- Outline objective benefits and drawbacks first.

PARTNERSHIP
- Do you intend to operate independently? You should then be familiar with the situation and co-ordinate with others.
- Working in association with a local Host promotes 'World Church' relationships and enhances the role of locals. (Westerners are well known for taking over or not letting go of any situation they can exert control over.)
- Partnership needs time, patience and love. It can be difficult, particularly if there is incompatibility from the start. When it works, it is better than independence.
- It can also involve Intermediaries and joint operations.

AUTHORITY
Policies and Procedures should be devised in advance, not least because these may have later legal implications.

Structures need to be considered to allow for:

Accountability	Chain of Authority
Decisiveness	Rapid Response
Responsibility	Knowledge Base
Commitment	Availability

Organisational Status may need defining, in the form of a Charity, Trust, Company, Association, etc.

ADMINISTRATION
You will need to provide for administrative support, in the form of staff (full or part-time), office space, communications devices

including a telephone and answering machine, typewriter, filing system (and possibly fax and computer). You may need to consider the legal aspects of employment and maintaining premises, as well as planning permission and Capital Gains Tax if operating from a private property. You will need venues for selection, training, orientation and follow up. Join an appropriate association such as the Evangelical Missionary Alliance and its new Short Term Programmes Functional Group.

REVIEW

Monitor what you do, audit outcomes against expectations and regularly remodel Policies, Procedures and Programmes.

MEMOS

Open a file on Organisational Structure. In it:

State your specific Aims and Objectives:

What do you want to do and is it reasonable?

What administrative facilities will you need and what complications do they bring?

Make extensive notes a) to devise specific Policies and Procedures and b) to allow for the Structural issues (and others you may think of).

TIMETABLE
- If you are setting up a new Programme without extensive experience and relevant contacts, allow at least one to two years until the Project, despite its apparent urgency.
- 'Lead times' for projects in 'Developing' countries may need to be extensive, given difficult communications, logistics and sometimes, different time-management.
- Start plans for future trips before current ones are over.

WORLD CHURCH ISSUES
- Understand the local church scene before you begin plans.
- Don't circumvent or compete with local initiatives.
- Beware of senseless denominationalism.
- Don't be misled by 'wolves in sheep's clothing'. Seek trusted references and offer your own, known to them.
- Link into the wider Missionary scene and learn from them.

AID VERSUS DEVELOPMENT
- Relief is a specialist area and shouldn't be attempted from scratch, from the outside. Obtain training.[1]
- Aid can promote superiority in the giver, dependency on the giver and reduce initiative in the receiver.
- Development seeks to treat causes, not effects; empowers and relies on locals and their structures; trains them, reducing the power of expatriates; networks and audits.[2]

FINANCE

External Audit of your accounts should be arranged, to maintain accountability (and any legal requirements).

Expenditure should be predicted accurately, with over-generous estimates when necessary. (See **PARTICIPANTS** section 2.2.2, **Fundraising** for most key areas to plan for.)

Income should be budgeted for realistically. If charging, see what other similar Organisations charge and what they include.

Over and Underspends should be anticipated; 10–20% over is reasonable. Also provide contingency funds to Teams.

Cash Flow must be forecast. It may plummet with flight costs then rise only later with Participant payments.

INSURANCE

Organiser's Liability should be accounted for, including money or materials handed over for Team use or return.

Travel and Medical insurance may be found for the Team via a broker (but don't then allow any personal policies, due to 'dual cover' rules). Or let them cover themselves, but inform you of details. (You may be wise to advise on minimum requirements or vet their policies before accepting them.)

LEGAL ISSUES

Legal Advice: **Seek it first.**

Blanket disclaimers are worthless. You still have some Common Law liabilities. A recent EC directive may also make Operators liable for negligence claims from Participants arising from Third Party action overseas.

Tour Operator Regulations of 1992 may or may not apply.

Data Protection Act should be followed if storing any identifiable personal information on computer.

In Loco Parentis status will be required for Minors. Legal problems defending charges of negligence can be enormous.

MEMOS

Open a file on the Working Context. In it:

Write, monitor and update a 'time-line' for your plans, highlighting deadlines. (NB: See 2.5.3 under **Medical Issues – PARTICIPANTS** for vaccination advice.) Consider a wall planner for a more visible record.

What further training or resources do you need, to assess and work with local problems overseas?

Draw up a cash flow forecast on a monthly basis and anticipate major fluxes in your account. Is it viable? Consider drawing on the skills of an accountant or business manager for more complex issues such as book-keeping, balance sheets and income/expenditure accounts.

What insurance do you think you and the Team need? Is this really sufficient?

What legal advice have you sought?

1 *Ian Davis and Michael Wall*, Christian Perspectives On Disaster Management, 1992, Tear Fund (UK) for Interchurch Relief and Development Alliance.
2 *Peter Batchelor*, People in Rural Development, 1993, 2nd edition, Paternoster Press, Carlisle.

Whether or not you plan to work in Europe, you would do well to read Working In Central and Eastern Europe.[1] Also, read the **PARTICIPANTS** section to prepare for more details.

PLANNING

Venue: What do you know about it? Is it appropriate?
Partnerships: What are the relationships and expectations?
Programme type: What are you trying to do?
Team: What make-up and leadership is needed and what size?
Timings: When? How long for? Does it overlap holidays, difficult seasons or significant dates, here or overseas?
Security: What issues need to be planned for?
Visits: Do you need to make a planning visit to aid administration and prevent misconceptions on both sides?
Communications: What will you rely on or use as a back up?
Work Plans/Supervision: What/who are they and how reliable?

LOGISTICS

Materials. Check availability, quality, price and delivery.
Shipping. Check cost, regulations and timing. Buying locally reduces transport costs and supports the local economy.
Local Transport. Are roads adequate and vehicles available?
Labour. Will you need to hire additional help at any point?

LIVING CONDITIONS

Hygiene. Are toilet and washing arrangements sufficient?
Food. Who will buy food, fuel and cook for the Team? Is it worth employing a local, who knows how to buy and cook local ingredients over local stoves/fires, etc.
Accommodation. Is it adequate and near enough to work/church?
Medical. What are the nearest appropriate facilities?

TRAVEL ARRANGEMENTS

See information for **LEADERS** under 3.2.1 **Practical Issues**.

International Flights. Talk to a travel specialist (see section on **RESOURCES**), as far before flying as possible, even if dates are not confirmed. They can make tentative bookings, advise on discounts, flexibility, reserve specific seats, offer a Visa service, insurance advice and 24 hour flight assistance. If you are not booking flights, provide everyone with comprehensively researched information on Visa requirements, useful travel specialists, booking deadlines and local travel details for arrival overseas.

Local Flights. You will have to book unscheduled flights directly, through local operators such as Missionary Aviation Fellowship. Sometimes these must be booked locally.

PRESS

See advice for **PARTICIPANTS** under 2.2.2 **Fundraising** and **LEADERS** under 3.2.5 **Emergencies**. Establish useful contacts and procedures.

EMERGENCIES

See **PARTICIPANTS** including 2.5.6 **Post-Trauma Stress** and **LEADERS** 3.2.5. Consider contacting the Foreign Office. Establish procedures in advance. Consider Critical Incident Debriefing.

MEMOS

Compile an Operations File covering each relevant issue.

1 Working in Central and Eastern Europe, 1994, Evangelical Missionary Alliance, London. (Price £1.00 – 32 pages).

PROMOTION

Read the section for **PARTICIPANTS**, to anticipate key issues.

Who do you want on your Programme? Are you setting up in response to a specific request, or will you have to find people to go on it? You will do well to consider all the opportunities now available. Take note of the **INTRODUCTION**.

When should you begin to advertise? Many Applicants don't begin thinking until Christmas/New Year for July/August.

What should you produce? Something relevant to your target group, with enough information for self-selection in or out.

Where should you advertise? For a country-wide catchment, consider the Short Term Service Directory.[1] With sufficient resources and a wide enough established mailing list, consider 'mail-shots' to your target groups.

How should material be produced? Balancing resources against need for Applicants, consider external design and printing. (NB Too little is as wasteful as too much, if no one goes.)

SELECTION

Read the section for **PARTICIPANTS** and **LEADERS**.

Participants. Beware of anti-discriminatory legislation, if offering services. Starting with your Aims, Objectives, Targets and operational needs, devise a specific 'Job Description' for the Team. From this, work out what you want in a member—the 'Person Specification'. Build up a system of application and selection from this, bearing in mind timing and finance. NB: Are you selecting out 'bad apples', or skimming off the 'cream'?

Leaders. Try to be objective and follow the same method as above. If organisational or 'political' considerations prevent this, you must at least avoid inappropriate choices.

PREPARATION

Written. See sections for **PARTICIPANTS** and **LEADERS** on what might be needed. Keep last season's information up to date.

Training. Provide adequate opportunities for Leaders.

Orientation. Bring the Team together for two days and nights (but more is better): a) to promote Team development, b) to offer additional information (the programme could be based on key topics from this book) and c) to spot problems *before* departure! Doing it immediately before flying keeps the Team together and reduces travel costs and forgotten information. An overseas orientation phase is a useful *addition*.

OVERSEAS PASTORAL CARE

Every Team and its Participants will have different needs. There are few situations where a Team should be expected to be totally self-contained. It is preferable to provide a local pastoral contact, with maturity and understanding, if only to help the Team in a difficult situation. Otherwise, they can help with local orientation and settling in.

FOLLOW UP

See sections for **PARTICIPANTS** and **LEADERS**. This is a key element of the experience and should not be skimped. A weekend reunion is an enjoyable opportunity for them.

MEMOS

Open a Personnel File. Make notes on policies relating to topics above:

1 The STS Directory, Christian Service Centre, Annual. See p. 137 for details.

Unlike the checklists for Participants and Leaders, this one is not a final check before 'take-off'. Your role is gradual and continuous and each issue should be regularly reviewed and amended. The issues below are key ones to have in your 'melting pot', at various stages. If you have not sufficiently considered one or more of them, or do not think they will be satisfactorily dealt with in time, I would counsel you to consider postponing plans. **Never rush, you're dealing with people's futures**:

Most recent Review Dates

Mission Statement	[ ]	[ ]	[ ]
Programme Aims	[ ]	[ ]	[ ]
Programme Objectives	[ ]	[ ]	[ ]
Programme Policies	[ ]	[ ]	[ ]
Programme Procedures	[ ]	[ ]	[ ]
Emergency Procedures	[ ]	[ ]	[ ]
Programme Viability	[ ]	[ ]	[ ]
Infrastructure	[ ]	[ ]	[ ]
Decision Making	[ ]	[ ]	[ ]
Timetabling	[ ]	[ ]	[ ]
Financial Systems	[ ]	[ ]	[ ]
Insurance Issues	[ ]	[ ]	[ ]
Legal Context	[ ]	[ ]	[ ]
Project Planning System	[ ]	[ ]	
Personnel Issues			
Promotion	[ ]	[ ]	[ ]
Selection	[ ]	[ ]	[ ]
Preparation	[ ]	[ ]	[ ]
Pastoral Care	[ ]	[ ]	[ ]
Follow Up	[ ]	[ ]	[ ]

Your Place within the World Church Environment
Development and Sustainability Issues
Systems for reviewing all the above

If you are unfamiliar with 'Western' culture and ways of working, it is hoped that the preceding sections will have opened your eyes a little. It is by no means a 'better' way of working. Also, it flows from a cushioned standard of living which is often (unfortunately) taken for granted. If your way of working is significantly different, the notes following are not intended to offend. They offer a glimpse of the way some 'Westerners' might approach issues.

AIMS AND OBJECTIVES

– Why does your Organisation exist and what is it doing?
– Do Short Term volunteers really fit into your objectives?

PARTNERSHIPS

– What are you hoping to achieve in Partnership? What are you hoping to offer? What are you hoping to receive? Are you feeling pressured and already overworked? Or is this just an opportunity to get 'something for nothing'?
– Do you feel an equal, or unhealthily dependent on them? Do they involve you, or use you to carry out their decisions?
– Stress what you can contribute in terms of educating and supervising the Team and providing administration.
– Be prepared to say 'No' before making commitments, if you don't feel decisions are suitable or didn't involve you.

WESTERN EXPECTATIONS AND LIMITATIONS

The following cultural notes on 'Westerners'[1] are only generalisations and not always true:

– They think that everything has a scientific explanation.
– They have limited experience of personal poverty or lack of 'essential' resources such as healthcare or transport.
– Efficiency and sticking to time schedules are often more important than greetings or relationships.
– They like spending time alone and privacy is important.
– They will try to reduce discomfort and inconvenience.
– They tend to judge themselves critically, against goals.
– They may be used to expressing close relationships physically, in public, by holding hands and hugging.

BENEFITS

– A Team of outsiders can often inject fresh encouragement.
– They may be able to help you achieve some of your goals such as building, administration, teaching, etc.

- You will have the opportunity to change wrong 'Western' attitudes by teaching what you want them to take home.
- You can contribute to increasing support for Mission, perhaps also stimulating a return to longer term Mission.

RESPONSIBILITY AND PASTORAL CARE

Most Short Term volunteers are young, inexperienced adults and will need help settling in and coping with a new culture and way of living, without the support they're used to.

REVIEW

It is well worth seriously asking yourself and others, if a project was worth it and should be repeated. It may not be.

MEMOS

It may be worth making notes relating to the relevant sections above.

1 *Margaret Wardell and Robin Thompson*, Entering Another's World, 1994, St John's Extension Studies, Nottingham, p.13.

PROJECT DEVELOPMENT
Timing

— You will know better than a foreigner, what time of year would be most suitable for you to receive a Team.
— You also know how long things may take to be arranged at your end. Don't be forced to go too fast.
— Feel able to postpone and cancel plans. However, it may be easier to negotiate a change in the work than the timing.

Work Supervision

— Where you know your requirements, don't be forced to have an expatriate supervisor. They may know nothing about local practices or contacts and sources of resources.
— Don't assume that skilled supervision can be provided. The right person can be very difficult to find here. Ask well in advance.
— Avoid misconceptions; see that someone responsible from your Organisation checks what the Team hope to do first.

Buffering the Community
Excepting Pioneering work, try to use understanding members of a community as buffers between outsiders and others in the community, either minimising or directly supervising contacts. Outsiders should be in supportive roles with locals directing operations.[1]

LOGISTICS
Materials. Know what you need, with adequate work plans.

Sources. Obtaining local supplies saves on shipping costs, import problems and helps the local economy. If requesting supplies to be sent in, be specific to avoid costly waste.

Transport. You will need to consider transport needs for people, materials and the state of the roads and the season!

LIVING CONDITIONS
Food and Drink. The Team should be keen to eat local food. However, they will need disinfected water, hygienic food preparation and advice on local hospitality, to avoid illness. They may need help with buying and cooking food.

Accommodation. Hotel facilities aren't needed. Screening against insects is useful. A nearby source of water, with means to disinfect it for washing is enough. Privacy in a hygienic toilet or latrine is expected. Security (locks or trusted watchmen) is needed, if local expectations are that 'Westerners' will be rich. Electricity is not always necessary, so long as adequate lighting can be supplied. Knowing what to expect is most important for a Team.

Location. Being close to work or with easy transport, is important, as is being near to the local church.

LOCAL ADMINISTRATION

You will need a postal address and street address for Team Visas. Sometimes they need an official letter of invitation from you. Access to a telephone and/or Fax will help.

RESOURCES

People. Will there be people available to meet and help the Team settle in? Will you also need temporary staff or labourers?

Finance. Teams cannot often bring or send much money for buildings. How will you obtain necessary funds and labour?

MEMOS

Make notes of what will be needed and what can be offered.

1 Saul and Pilar Cruz, Armonia Project, Mexico City. 'Buffer Model' from a Presentation on Christian Urban Community Development, in July 1995, Kuala Lumpur, Malaysia.

As with the checklist for Organisers, the following are important issues to constantly bear in mind and plan for. However, as with the Participants and Leaders, the 'day of reckoning' will come, when the Team will arrive to the preparation you have made!

Aims and Objectives

Partnerships

An understanding of 'Westerners'

Pastoral Care issues

Project initiation acceptable

Timing agreed

Work supervision understood

Logistics planned

Living conditions considered

Local administration arranged

Resources sufficient

Reviews of above

General Books

The Short Term Mission Handbook—A Comprehensive Guide for Participants and Leaders, First edition, 1992, Berry Publishing Services Inc., 701 Main Street, Evanston, IL60202, USA. (This is an interesting series of articles, which appears to concentrate predominantly on the rationale for Short Term Mission. Despite the title, it offers minimal practical advice, but can help you ask whether you really should be applying. The publishers hoped to produce a new edition every three years, so a new one was due in 1995.)

Stepping Out—A Guide to Short Term Missions, Editors: Tim Gibson, Steve Hawthorne, Richard Krekel and Kn Moy. Updated and reprinted, 1992, YWAM Publishing, PO Box 55787, Seattle, WA98155, USA. (This is another collection of short contributions, practical in nature, concentrating more than the book above on detailed issues. However, it is anecdotal and by no means comprehensive—more of an appetite whetter. It does give more background on intangible issues such as relationships and personal spiritual issues, than I have.)

Prepared To Serve—A practical guide to Christian service overseas. Editor: Derek Williams, 1989, Tear Fund/Scripture Union. (Out of print but mostly absorbed into the next reference.) This collection of essays was collated for long-term workers but has many useful insights for short-termers. Again, these tend to be anecdotal or relate to personal rather than practical preparation.)

Entering Another's World—A Workbook for Those who Want to Learn How to Live for God in Another Culture, Margaret Wardell and Robin Thompson, 1994, St John's Extension Studies, Bramcote, Nottingham, NG9 3DS. (This is a valuable study guide, which can be bought alone, or used as part of a larger, tutored, open-learning Mission Studies course called Culture To Culture, through St John's College. It amplifies and encourages personal reflection on a wide range of topics relevant to personal—though not practical—preparation.)

The World Christian—A Workbook for Those Aiming to Take the Gospel from Culture to Culture, Robin Thompson, 1992, St John's Extension Studies/Lynx Communications. (This is another independent component of the Culture To Culture course, giving useful insights into the current state of the World Church and approaches to evangelism within other religious contexts.)

Human Development Report, (Annual), United Nations Development Programme, Oxford University Press, Oxford. (Statistics on poorer countries' development status.)

Operation World, Patrick Johnstone, 1994, OM Publishing, Carlisle. (Uniquely valuable country by country prayer and statistics guide.)

The World's Religions—A Lion Handbook, 1982, Lion Publishing, Tring. (Invaluable guide, from a balanced Christian perspective.)

Healthy Beyond Heathrow, Ted Lankester, 1994, Interhealth, London. (Thorough yet portable lay-person's guide to personal healthcare overseas.)

Specific Planning Books

The Lonely Planet Guides. (Useful specific information on culture, language, history, politics, climate, geography, city centre maps, places to stay, travel details etc. for many specific countries.)

The Traveller's Handbook, 1994, WEXAS, London. (Incredibly useful mine of practical information and addresses for independent travellers of all types.)

Working In Central And Eastern Europe—Guidelines for Christians, 1994, Evangelical Missionary Alliance, London. (Useful tips specific to this region, but a good model for questions you might need to ask before organising a trip anywhere.)

Short Term Christian Medical Service Overseas, 1994, Christian Medical Fellowship/Medical Missionary Association, 157 Waterloo Road, London SE1 8XN. (Useful guide to finding placements and preparing yourself, if you are a doctor.)

STS Directory—World-Wide opportunities for Short-Term Christian Service, Annual, The Christian Service Centre, Holloway Street West, Lower Gornal, Dudley, West Midlands, DY3 2DZ. (The main collated source for those wishing to advertise or find such programmes, with some advice.)

Christian Perspectives On Disaster Management, Ian Davis and Michael Wall, 1992, Tear Fund, London, for IRDA—The Interchurch Relief and Development Alliance. (A useful guide to key issues.)

The UK Christian Handbook, Editors: Peter Brierley, Val Hiscock, David Longley, Annual, Christian Research Association/Evangelical Alliance/Bible Society. (Comprehensive guide to addresses of Christian organisations, publishers, services etc. in the UK.)

Re-Entry—Making the Transition from Missions to Life at Home, Peter Jordan, 1992, YWAM Associates International, PO Box 35021, Vancouver, B.C. V6M 4G1, Canada. (Helpful advice, particularly for long-termers, on returning home.)

The Evangelical Alliance (EA), Whitefield House, 186 Kennington Park Road, London SE11 4BT.

The Evangelical Missionary Alliance (EMA), (Same address).

The Short Term Functional Group, (Part of the EMA).

Services

Healthcare

Interhealth, 157 Waterloo Road, London SE1 8US. Phone 0171–902 9000. (Can provide medical screening, advice, medical kits and supplies and a 24-hour overseas advice facility for clients.)

Care For Missions, Ellem Lodge, Duns, Berwickshire, TD11 3SG. Phone 013617 677. Fax 013617 329. (A sister organisation to Interhealth providing facilities to Scotland and the North.)

Travel Agents

Key Travel, 92–96 Eversholt Street, London NW1 1BP. Phone 0171–387 4933. Fax 0171–387 1090. (Highly experienced, very helpful specialist agent for complex and charity itineraries in 'Third World' settings, with a 24 hour telephone assistance service for clients overseas.)

WEXAS, 45–49 Brompton Road, Knightsbridge, London, SW3 1DE. Phone 0171–581 8632. Fax 0171–589 1104. (Specialist travel club, able to offer an excellent personal service, often with very cheap flights, particularly on less complex routes.)

Commercial insurers

Bain Hogg, c/o Ian Lee, UK Division, LMS House, Riverway Estate, Portsmouth Road, Guildford, Surrey, GU3 1NJ. Phone 01483–505000. Fax 01483–36821. (Can arrange tailored insurance packages for organisation—but not individuals.)

Solicitors

Lewis and Dick, c/o Alistair Watson, 443 Kingston Road, Ewell, Surrey, KT19 0DG. Phone 0181–393 0055. Fax 0181–393 3317. (Solicitors with specific experience advising missions and short-term programme organisers.)

Shipping and Non-medical Equipment

Mission Supplies, Alpha Place, Garth Road, Morden, Surrey, SM4 4LX. Phone 0181–337 0161. Fax 0181–337 7220. (Shipping agents, used by many charities and missionaries. Can also supply equipment such as water filters etc.)

Unimatco, Beta Works, Tatling End, Gerrards Cross, Bucks, SL9 7BB. Phone 01753–881605. Fax 01753–889378. (See above.)

Medical Supplies

ECHO, Ullswater Crescent, Coulsdon, Surrey CR3 2HR. Phone 0181–660 2220. Fax 0181–668 0751. (Suppliers of hospital equipment and drugs for charitable use overseas. Can advise on essential drugs and equipment for supply to hospitals and in disasters, etc.)

Notes to the Index
1. Urgent Issues are <u>UNDERLINED, BOLD AND IN CAPITALS</u>.
2. Section Headings are <u>UNDERLINED AND IN CAPITALS</u>.
3. Page and Chapter Headings are IN CAPITALS where appropriate.
4. Other Topics are in Lower Case and often important.

MEMO

MEMO

MEMO

MEMO